HOW TO START A HOME-BASED COLLECTION AGENCY

Robert H. Bills

Eatonbrook Publishing

Published by: Eatonbrook Publishing
6 Mann Drive, Liverpool, N.Y. 13088

Cover design by Ben Carpenter: www.bc2design.com

ISBN: 0-9728430-0-0

Library of Congress Control Number: 2003101704

Visit us at: www.YourCollectionAgency.com

Printed in the United States of America

Acknowledgements

I would like to dedicate this book to four people for their inspiration, guidance and support in writing this book.

To my father, Ray Bills, who taught me the ABC's of collections and the instilled the importance of business ethics within me.

To my mother, Gwen Bills, whose kindness and warmth taught me the importance of being able to empathize with others.

To my daughter, Mandy Dolson, for being a constant reminder of how quickly time passes, thereby encouraging me to take action.

To my amazing wife, Jean Ann, whose love, support and encouragement made this book possible. No husband has ever had a better friend.

Table of Contents

Introduction

How To Start A Home-Based Collection Agency will give you more than the usual platitudes and sterile rehashed insights of home-based professionals *telling* you how to start a home-based collection business, but not *showing* you how to do it. There is a difference.

This book will provide you with easy to understand step-by-step strategies to successfully launch and grow your own collection business. You may just possibly reduce the number of your own mistakes, by listening to someone who can say – Been There. Done That.

Have you ever noticed the number of *"How To Start A Home-Based Business"* type books begin with such sage advice as: "Be sure to find your own space within your home to set up shop and avoid the kitchen area"?

Please excuse the sarcasm, but if you need an "expert" to explain you can't effectively run a collection agency (or almost any business) from your kitchen table, you might want to re-think your entrepreneurial plans.

"Necessity is the Mother of Invention"

For many years I owned and operated a well-established mom-and-pop small loan company. Somewhat reminiscent of the company run by the character George Bailey in the 1946 Christmas classic, "It's a Wonderful Life."

Our niche was lending small amounts of money ($800-1500) on a mostly secured basis to people with special needs. These individuals may have had a credit problem, no credit or simply liked doing business with us. We worked with them in good times and bad times. Banks were not exactly targeting these people for loans or fresh-starts. These were the 60's, 70's and 80's.

Fast forward to the 90's

Guess what?

Despite slow credit or a recent bankruptcy, large regional banks started giving "our" customers unsecured credit cards with limits of $3500-5000. Billion dollar banks and finance companies began to expand their services and ease of access to cash. Large auto dealers set up specific departments to help credit-challenged individuals.

INTRODUCTION

Bankruptcies soared. Total U.S. bankruptcy filings went from 348,521 in 1984 to 1,178,555 in 1996. According to the Administrative Office of the U.S. Courts bankruptcy filings surpassed 1.5 million for the first time for the 12-month period ending June 30, 2002.

Add to this scenario a relentless consolidation of all finance companies. Suddenly, a lending license once valued at several thousand dollars was essentially worthless. Industry consolidation had also dried up the number of potential buyers for our receivables. Competitors had now developed their own sophisticated underwriting technology and weren't really interested in accepting accounts outside their lending parameters. I could go on, but you get the idea. Things change.

The truth was unavoidable – our day had come and gone. If I immediately liquidated receivables, unsecured investors would have been nearly wiped out. I was determined to act in their best interest regardless of the impact on my personal finances and implemented an orderly termination plan.

It was just about at this time the "mother of my invention" gave birth. Self-examination revealed an executive, 49 years old, with a long track record of self-employment. It was clear I would not likely be on the hit parade of most human resource managers. Of course, being broke and emotionally stressed didn't help my situation either.

So what could I do with 30 years of credit / collection and insurance claim experience?

The bells went off in my head!!! I would make my own opportunity. I would start my own collection agency and perhaps branch off into medical billing and accounts receivable management.

> "There is no security on this earth, there is only opportunity."
>
> — General Douglas MacArthur (1880 - 1964)

Within 12 months

Within 12 months I found myself collecting accounts for a variety of businesses. Here is a small sample:

• Precision sheet metal fabricator
• An environmental service company
• Canadian manufacturer
• Doctors
• Waste management firm
• A property management company
• An executive housing establishment in England

Perhaps this book will help you learn and profit from my mistakes and speed you on the road to success...let our journey to starting your home-based collection agency begin.

> "The man who makes no mistakes does not usually make anything."
>
> — Bishop W.C. McGee

Chapter 1: The Right Stuff

Before we get to the fun stuff, lets take a minute to see if you have "The Right Stuff" to succeed in starting your own collection agency.

Experience

While experience in the collection industry would be a big plus – it is not an absolute. If you lack collection experience, you might want to consider working part-time for a local agency. Many large collection agencies need extra help during evening hours and on weekends. Look at it as an opportunity to go to school and get paid. Of course, this may not be an option for you.

Misconceptions

Individuals new to the collection industry sometimes have a misconception of what it means to be a collector. This perception is partially reinforced when some collection agencies advertise themselves as being tough on "deadbeats" and approach clients with a "we get the money no matter what, no excuses" philosophy. They use fear, guilt and intimidation to get paid.

I can't think of a more depressing or reprehensible way to make a living. Do you honestly think the majority of debtors enjoy getting a dunning notice or collection phone call?

Abraham Lincoln liked to tell the story of a man called upon to witness at a church meeting and said, "When I do good I feel good, when I do bad I feel bad, and that's my religion." You should always feel good about your chosen profession.

Poop Happens

For the most part, I have found debtors to be delinquent because of a change in personal or business circumstances. They are not calculating individuals or companies that set out to cheat your client. Simply put: "poop happens." Individuals and companies can quickly find themselves facing unforeseen problems. Good people lose jobs and get divorced. A serious illness can leave someone drowning in medical bills.

Companies can run into problems with their suppliers and customers. Many companies have cash flow problems that temporarily prevent them from paying as originally agreed because...their own customers have not paid "them". These are golden opportunities. If handled correctly, you will collect the debt and more importantly acquire a new client.

Have you ever faced difficult financial times? If you have been through your own troubled times, it will increase your ability to nurture a debtor or business owners self-esteem thereby increasing your chances of a successful collection. There is no typical debtor. "Your" attitude can have a defining impact on cooperation and the willingness of a debtor to pay.

Primary Skills

There are two primary skills you **must** have to succeed:

Communication Skills – You will need the ability to effectively communicate in person, by mail and over the internet. You must be a good listener. You can't begin to solve a debtor or client problem without fully understanding a given situation.

Investigative Skills – You will be expected to search out and uncover data related to corporate ownership, assets, bankruptcies, UCC filings, tax liens, domain names and much more.

Women

In my opinion, women generally make the best collectors. I base this statement on decades of working primarily with or for women. Women have an innate ability to empathize. Women are excellent at "the details". Debt collection requires a lot of tedious research.

Women can be tough when necessary, but don't seem to feel the need to always demonstrate their toughness. Of course, men can be excellent collectors and not every woman fits the preceding description, but this has been my general observation.

One Question

Before setting up shop, ask yourself – why you want to start a collection agency. Is it a matter of necessity, as it was in my case? Is this a long time dream? Are you seeking a supplemental income? The stronger your reason and desire, the better your chance for success.

Chapter 2: What Is a Collection Agency?

A collection agency is a third-party collector of past-due receivables. Accounts are referred to agencies by a variety of businesses. Credit card companies, banks, credit unions, retail stores, healthcare providers all use collection agencies. Essentially any business that extends credit is a potential collection agency client.

Think About It

Financial institutions and other businesses are busy enough trying to service the needs and wants of current customers. Does it really make sense for them to spend time skip tracing accounts that are more then 6 months delinquent? Should a doctor's staff spend time acting as a collection agency and alienating some patients?

A third-party collection agency can do all the grunt work utilizing collection techniques reflective of a particular client professional image. A collection agency can be a "buffer" between a client and a debtor. Many times a client wants to be paid and keep the customer/patient.

Statistics

According to the Bureau on Labor Statistics, 2000-2001 Occupational Outlook Handbook employment in the collection industry is expected to grow 35% or more by 2008.

Chapter 3: The Business Plan – Road Map to Success

There are numerous software products available to help you document your business plan, evaluate your marketing strategy, and test your product ideas. You will find hundreds of web sites dedicated to business plans by simply searching the major directories and search engines.

A Tutorial and Self-paced Activity

Business Plan Outline

Below is an outline for a business plan. Use this model as a guide when developing the business plan for your business.

Elements of a Business Plan

I. Cover sheet

II. Statement of purpose

III. Table of contents

IV. The Business

    A. Description of business

    B. Marketing

    C. Competition

    D. Operating procedures

    E. Personnel

    F. Business insurance

    G. Financial data

V. Financial Data

    A. Loan applications

    B. Capital equipment and supply list

    C. Balance sheet

    D. Breakeven analysis

    E. Pro-forma income projections (profit & loss statements)

        1. Three-year summary

        2. Detail by month, first year

        3. Detail by quarters, second and third years

        4. Assumptions upon which projections were based

    F. Pro-forma cash flow

        Follow guidelines for letter E.

CHAPTER 3: THE BUSINESS PLAN - ROAD MAP TO SUCCESS

VI. Supporting Documents
   A. Tax returns of principals for last three years
   B. Personal financial statement (all banks have these forms)
   C. In the case of a franchised business, a copy of franchise contract and all supporting documents provided by the franchisor
   D. Copy of proposed lease or purchase agreement for building space
   E. Copy of licenses and other legal documents
   F. Copy of resumes of all principals
   G. Copies of letters of intent from suppliers, etc.

The Business Plan - What It Includes

What goes in a business plan? This is an excellent question. And, it is one that many new and potential small business owners should ask, but oftentimes don't ask. The body of the business plan can be divided into four distinct sections: 1) the description of the business, 2) the marketing plan, 3) the financial management plan and 4) the management plan. Addenda to the business plan should include the executive summary, supporting documents and financial projections.

The Business Plan - Description Of The Business

In this section, provide a detailed description of your business. An excellent question to ask yourself is: "What business am I in?" In answering this question include your products, market and services as well as a thorough description of what makes your business unique. Remember, however, that as you develop your business plan, you may have to modify or revise your initial questions.

The business description section is divided into three primary sections. Section 1 actually describes your business, Section 2 the product or service you will be offering and Section 3 the location of your business, and why this location is desirable (if you have a franchise, some franchisors assist in site selection).

When describing your business, generally you should explain:

1. Legalities - business form: proprietorship, partnership, corporation. The licenses or permits you will need.

2. Business type: merchandizing, manufacturing or service.

3. What your product or service is.

4. Is it a new independent business, a takeover, an expansion, a franchise?

5. Why your business will be profitable. What are the growth opportunities? Will franchising impact on growth opportunities?

6. When your business will be open (days, hours)?

7. What you have learned about your kind of business from outside sources (trade suppliers, bankers, other franchise owners, franchisor, publications).

A cover sheet goes before the description. It includes the name, address and telephone number of the business and the names of all principals. In the description of your business, describe the unique aspects and how or why they will appeal to consumers. Emphasize any special features that you feel will appeal to customers and explain how and why these features are appealing.

The description of your business should clearly identify goals and objectives and it should clarify why you are, or why you want to be, in business.

The Business Plan - Product/Service

Try to describe the benefits of your goods and services from your customers' perspective. Successful business owners know or at least have an idea of what their customers want or expect from them. This type of anticipation can be helpful in building customer satisfaction and loyalty. And, it certainly is a good strategy for beating the competition or retaining your competitiveness. Describe:

1. What you are selling.

2. How your product or service will benefit the customer.

3. Which products/services are in demand; if there will be a steady flow of cash.

4. What is different about the product or service your business is offering.

The Business Plan - 3. The Location

The location of your business can play a decisive role in its success or failure. Your location should be built around your customers, it should be accessible and it should provide a sense of security. Consider these questions when addressing this section of your business plan:

CHAPTER 3: *THE BUSINESS PLAN - ROAD MAP TO SUCCESS*

1. What are your location needs?

2. What kind of space will you need?

3. Why is the area desirable? the building desirable?

4. Is it easily accessible? Is public transportation available? Is street lighting adequate?

5. Are market shifts or demographic shifts occurring?

It may be a good idea to make a checklist of questions you identify when developing your business plan. Categorize your questions and, as you answer each question, remove it from your list.

The Business Plan - The Marketing Plan

Marketing plays a vital role in successful business ventures. How well you market you business, along with a few other considerations, will ultimately determine your degree of success or failure. The key element of a successful marketing plan is to know your customers-their likes, dislikes, expectations. By identifying these factors, you can develop a marketing strategy that will allow you to arouse and fulfill their needs.

Identify your customers by their age, sex, income/educational level and residence. At first, target only those customers who are more likely to purchase your product or service. As your customer base expands, you may need to consider modifying the marketing plan to include other customers.

Develop a marketing plan for your business by answering these questions. (Potential franchise owners will have to use the marketing strategy the franchisor has developed.) Your marketing plan should be included in your business plan and contain answers to the questions outlined below.

1. Who are your customers? Define your target market(s).

2. Are your markets growing? steady? declining?

3. Is your market share growing? steady? declining?

4. If a franchise, how is your market segmented?

5. Are your markets large enough to expand?

6. How will you attract, hold, increase your market share? If a franchise, will the franchisor provide assistance in this area? Based on the franchisor's strategy? how will you promote your sales?

7. What pricing strategy have you devised?

Appendix I contains a sample Marketing Plan and Marketing Tips, Tricks and Traps, a condensed guide on how to market your product or service. Study these documents carefully when developing the marketing portion of your business plan.

The Business Plan - Competition

Competition is a way of life. We compete for jobs, promotions, scholarships to institutes of higher learning, in sports-and in almost every aspect of your lives. Nations compete for the consumer in the global marketplace as do individual business owners. Advances in technology can send the profit margins of a successful business into a tailspin causing them to plummet overnight or within a few hours. When considering these and other factors, we can conclude that business is a highly competitive, volatile arena. Because of this volatility and competitiveness, it is important to know your competitors.

Questions like these can help you:

1. Who are your five nearest direct competitors?

2. Who are your indirect competitors?

3. How are their businesses: steady? increasing? decreasing?

4. What have you learned from their operations? from their advertising?

5. What are their strengths and weaknesses?

6. How does their product or service differ from yours?

Start a file on each of your competitors. Keep manila envelopes of their advertising and promotional materials and their pricing strategy techniques. Review these files periodically, determining when and how often they advertise, sponsor promotions and offer sales. Study the copy used in the advertising and promotional materials, and their sales strategy. For example, is their copy short? descriptive? catchy? or how much do they reduce prices for sales? Using this technique can help you to understand your competitors better and how they operate their businesses.

CHAPTER 3: *THE BUSINESS PLAN - ROAD MAP TO SUCCESS*

The Business Plan - Pricing and Sales

Your pricing strategy is another marketing technique you can use to improve your overall competitiveness. Get a feel for the pricing strategy your competitors are using. That way you can determine if your prices are in line with competitors in your market area and if they are in line with industry averages.

Some of the pricing strategies are:
• retail cost and pricing
• competitive position
• pricing below competition
• pricing above competition
• price lining
• multiple pricing
• service costs and pricing (for service businesses only)
• service components
• material costs
• labor costs
• overhead costs

The key to success is to have a well-planned strategy, to establish your policies and to constantly monitor prices and operating costs to ensure profits. Even in a franchise where the franchisor provides operational procedures and materials, it is a good policy to keep abreast of the changes in the marketplace because these changes can affect your competitiveness and profit margins.

Appendix 1 contains a sample Price/Quality Matrix, review it for ideas on pricing strategies for your competitors. Determine which of the strategies they use, if it is effective and why it is effective.

The Business Plan - Advertising and Public Relations

How you advertise and promote your goods and services may make or break your business. Having a good product or service and not advertising and promoting it is like not having a business at all. Many business owners operate under the mistaken concept that the business will promote itself, and channel money that should be used for advertising and promotions to other areas of the business. Advertising and promotions, however, are the life line of a business and should be treated as such.

Devise a plan that uses advertising and networking as a means to promote your business. Develop short, descriptive copy (text material) that clearly identifies your goods or services, its location and price. Use catchy phrases to arouse the interest of your readers, listeners or viewers. In the case of a franchise, the franchisor will provide advertising and promotional materials as part of the franchise package, you may need approval to use any materials that you and your staff develop. Whether or not this is the case, as a courtesy, allow the franchisor the opportunity to review, comment on and, if required, approve these materials before using them. Make sure the advertisements you create are consistent with the image the franchisor is trying to project. Remember the more care and attention you devote to your marketing program, the more successful your business will be.

A more detailed explanation of the marketing plan and how to develop an effective marketing program is provided in the Workshop on Marketing. See Training Module 3 - Marketing Your Business for Success.

The Business Plan - The Management Plan

Managing a business requires more than just the desire to be your own boss. It demands dedication, persistence, the ability to make decisions and the ability to manage both employees and finances. Your management plan, along with your marketing and financial management plans, sets the foundation for and facilitates the success of your business.

Like plants and equipment, people are resources-they are the most valuable asset a business has. You will soon discover that employees and staff will play an important role in the total operation of your business. Consequently, it's imperative that you know what skills you possess and those you lack since you will have to hire personnel to supply the skills that you lack. Additionally, it is imperative that you know how to manage and treat your employees. Make them a part of the team. Keep them informed of, and get their feedback regarding, changes. Employees oftentimes have excellent ideas that can lead to new market areas, innovations to existing products or services or new product lines or services which can improve your overall competitiveness.

Your management plan should answer questions such as:
• How does your background/business experience help you in this business?
• What are your weaknesses and how can you compensate for them?
• Who will be on the management team?
• What are their strengths/weaknesses?
• What are their duties?
• Are these duties clearly defined?
• If a franchise, what type of assistance can you expect from the franchisor?
• Will this assistance be ongoing?

CHAPTER 3: *THE BUSINESS PLAN - ROAD MAP TO SUCCESS*

• What are your current personnel needs?
• What are your plans for hiring and training personnel?
• What salaries, benefits, vacations, holidays will you offer? If a franchise, are these issues covered in the management package the franchisor will provide?
• What benefits, if any, can you afford at this point?

If a franchise, the operating procedures, manuals and materials devised by the franchisor should be included in this section of the business plan. Study these documents carefully when writing your business plan, and be sure to incorporate this material. The franchisor should assist you with managing your franchise. Take advantage of their expertise and develop a management plan that will ensure the success for your franchise and satisfy the needs and expectations of employees, as well as the franchisor.

The Business Plan - The Financial Management Plan

Sound financial management is one of the best ways for your business to remain profitable and solvent. How well you manage the finances of your business is the cornerstone of every successful business venture. Each year thousands of potentially successful businesses fail because of poor financial management. As a business owner, you will need to identify and implement policies that will lead to and ensure that you will meet your financial obligations.

To effectively manage your finances, plan a sound, realistic budget by determining the actual amount of money needed to open your business (start-up costs) and the amount needed to keep it open (operating costs). The first step to building a sound financial plan is to devise a start-up budget. Your start-up budget will usually include such one-time-only costs as major equipment, utility deposits, down payments, etc.

The start-up budget should allow for these expenses.

Start-up Budget:
• personnel (costs prior to opening)
• legal/professional fees
• occupancy
• licenses/permits
• equipment
• insurance
• supplies
• advertising/promotions
• salaries/wages

• accounting
• income
• utilities
• payroll expenses

An operating budget is prepared when you are actually ready to open for business. The operating budget will reflect your priorities in terms of how your spend your money, the expenses you will incur and how you will meet those expenses (income). Your operating budget also should include money to cover the first three to six months of operation. It should allow for the following expenses.

Operating Budget:
• personnel
• insurance
• rent
• depreciation
• loan payments
• advertising/promotions
• legal/accounting
• miscellaneous expenses
• supplies
• payroll expenses
• salaries/wages
• utilities
• dues/subscriptions/fees
• taxes
• repairs/maintenance

The financial section of your business plan should include any loan applications you've filed, a capital equipment and supply list, balance sheet, breakeven analysis, pro-forma income projections (profit and loss statement) and pro-forma cash flow. The income statement and cash flow projections should include a three-year summary, detail by month for the first year, and detail by quarter for the second and third years.

The accounting system and the inventory control system that you will be using is generally addressed in this section of the business plan also. If a franchise, the franchisor may stipulate in the franchise contract the type of accounting and inventory systems you may use. If this is the case, he or she should have a system already intact and you will be required to adopt this system. Whether you develop the accounting and inventory systems yourself, have an outside financial advisor develop the systems or the franchisor provides these systems, you will need to acquire a thorough

CHAPTER 3: *THE BUSINESS PLAN - ROAD MAP TO SUCCESS*

understanding of each segment and how it operates. Your financial advisor can assist you in developing this section of your business plan.

The following questions should help you determine the amount of start-up capital you will need to purchase and open a franchise.
• How much money do you have?
• How much money will you need to purchase the franchise?
• How much money will you need for start-up?
• How much money will you need to stay in business?

Other questions that you will need to consider are:
• What type of accounting system will your use? Is it a single entry or dual entry system?
• What will your sales goals and profit goals for the coming year be? If a franchise, will the franchisor set your sales and profit goals? Or, will he or she expect you to reach and retain a certain sales level and profit margin?
• What financial projections will you need to include in your business plan?
• What kind of inventory control system will you use?

Your plan should include an explanation of all projections. Unless you are thoroughly familiar with financial statements, get help in preparing your cash flow and income statements and your balance sheet. Your aim is not to become a financial wizard, but to understand the financial tools well enough to gain their benefits. Your accountant or financial advisor can help you accomplish this goal.

Sample balance sheets, income projections (profit and loss statements) and cash flow statements are included in Appendix 2, Financial Management. For a detailed explanation of these and other more complex financial concepts, contact your local SBA Office. Look under the U.S. Government section of the local telephone directory.

CHAPTER 3: *THE BUSINESS PLAN - ROAD MAP TO SUCCESS*

Self-paced Activity

During this activity you will:
• Briefly describe what goes into a business plan.
• Identify advantages of developing the marketing, management and financial management plans.
• List financial projections included in the financial management plan.
• Sketch an outline for a business plan.

Appendix 1

Marketing

1. The Marketing Plan
2. Price/quality Matrix
3. Marketing Tips, Tricks & Traps

THE ENTREPRENEUR'S MARKETING PLAN

This is the marketing plan of _____

I. MARKET ANALYSIS
    A. Target Market - Who are the customers?
        1. We will be selling primarily to (check all that apply and write total percent of business to the right):
            ❑ Private sector _____
            ❑ Wholesalers _____
            ❑ Retailers _____
            ❑ Government _____
            ❑ Other _____
        2. We will be targeting customers by:
            a. Product line/services. We will target specific lines _____
            b. Geographic area? Which areas?_____
            c. Sales? We will target sales of _____
            d. Industry? Our target industry is _____
            e. Other? _____
        3. How much will our selected market spend on our type of product or service this coming year? $ _____
    B. Competition
        1. Who are our competitors?
            Name _____

CHAPTER 3: *THE BUSINESS PLAN - ROAD MAP TO SUCCESS*

Address_____

Years In Business _____

Market Share _____

Price/strategy_____

Product/service _____

Features _____

Name _____

Address_____

Years In Business _____

Market Share _____

Price/strategy_____

Product/service _____

Features _____

2. How competitive is the market? (check one)

    ❏ High

    ❏ Medium

    ❏ Low

3. List below your strengths and weaknesses compared to your competition (consider such areas as location, size of resources, reputation, services, personnel, etc.):

Strengths	Weaknesses
1._____	1. _____
2._____	2. _____
3._____	3. _____
4._____	4. _____

C. Environment

    1. The following are some important economic factors that will affect our product or service (such as trade area growth, industry health, economic trends, taxes, rising energy prices, etc.):

      _____

      _____

      _____

    2. The following are some important legal factors that will affect our market:

      _____

      _____

      _____

    3. The following are some important government factors:

      _____

      _____

4. The following are other environmental factors that will affect our market, but over which we have no control:

_____

_____

_____

II. PRODUCT OR SERVICE ANALYSIS

A. Description

1. Describe here what the product/service is and what it does:

_____

_____

_____

B. Comparison

1. What advantages does our product/service have over those of the competition (consider such things as unique features, patents, expertise, special training, etc.)?

_____

_____

_____

2. What disadvantages does it have?

_____

_____

_____

C. Some Considerations

1. Where will you get your materials and supplies?

_____

_____

_____

2. List other considerations:

_____

_____

_____

III. MARKETING STRATEGIES - MARKET MIX

A. Image

1. First, what kind of image do we want to have (such as cheap but good, or exclusiveness, or customer-oriented or highest quality, or convenience, or speed, or ...)?

_____

B. Features

1. List the features we will emphasize:

a. _____

CHAPTER 3: *THE BUSINESS PLAN - ROAD MAP TO SUCCESS*

    b. _____

    c. _____

C. Pricing

    1. We will be using the following pricing strategy:

       ❏ Markup on cost. What % markup? _____

       ❏ Suggested price

       ❏ Competitive

       ❏ Below competition

       ❏ Premium price

       ❏ Other _____

    2. Are our prices in line with our image?

       ❏ Yes   ❏ No

    3. Do our prices cover costs and leave a margin of profit?

       ❏ Yes   ❏ No

D. Customer Services

    1. List the customer services we provide:

       a. _____

       b. _____

       c. _____

    2. These are our sales/credit terms:

       a. _____

       b. _____

       c. _____

    3. The competition offers the following services:

       a. _____

       b. _____

       c. _____

E. Advertising/Promotion

    1. These are the things we wish to say about the business:

       _____

       _____

       _____

    2. We will use the following advertising/promotion sources:

       ❏ Television

       ❏ Radio

       ❏ Direct mail

       ❏ Personal contacts

       ❏ Trade associations

       ❏ Newspaper

❏ Magazines
❏ Yellow Pages
❏ Billboard
❏ Other _____

3. The following are the reasons why we consider the media we have chosen to be the most effective:

_____

_____

_____

Marketing Tips, Tricks & Traps

I. Marketing Steps
   A. Classifying Your Customers' Needs
   B. Targeting Your Customer(s)
   C. Examining Your "Niche"
   D. Identifying Your Competitors
   E. Assessing and Managing Your Available Resources
      1. Financial
      2. Human
      3. Material
      4. Production

Notes and strategies for your business:

_____

_____

_____

II. Marketing Positioning
   A. Follower versus Leader
   B. Quality versus Price
   C. Innovator versus Adaptor
   D. Customer versus Product
   E. International versus Domestic
   F. Private Sector versus Government

Notes and strategies for your business:

_____

_____

_____

CHAPTER 3: *THE BUSINESS PLAN - ROAD MAP TO SUCCESS*

III. Sales Strategy
  A. Use Customer-Oriented Selling Approach - By Constructing Agreement
    1. Phase One: Establish Rapport with Customer - by agreeing to discuss what the customer wants to achieve.
    2. Phase Two: Determine Customer Objective and Situational Factors - by agreeing on what the customer wants to achieve and those factors in the environment that will influence these results.
    3. Phase Three: Recommend a Customer Action Plan - by agreeing that using your product/ service will indeed achieve what customer wants.
    4. Phase Four: Obtaining Customer Commitment - By agreeing that the customer will acquire your product/service.
  B. Emphasize Customer Advantage
    1. Must be Read: When a competitive advantage can not be demonstrated, it will not translate into a benefit.
    2. Must be Important to the Customer: When the perception of competitive advantage varies between supplier and customer, the customer wins.
    3. Must be Specific: When a competitive advantage lacks specificity, it translates into mere puffery and is ignored.
    4. Must be Promotable: When a competitive advantage is proven, it is essential that your customer know it, lest it not exist at all.
Notes and strategies for your business:

_____

_____

_____

IV. Benefits vs. Features
  A. The six "O's" of organizing Customer Buying Behavior
    1. ORIGINS of purchase: Who buys it?
    2. OBJECTIVES of purchase: What do they need/buy?
    3. OCCASIONS of purchase: When do they buy it?
    4. OUTLETS of purchase: Where do they buy it?
    5. OBJECTIVES of purchase: Why do they buy it?
    6. OPERATIONS of purchase: How do they buy it?
  B. Convert features to benefits using the "...Which Means..."
  C. Transition
  C. Sales Maxim: "Unless the proposition appeals to their INTEREST, unless it satisfies their DESIRES, and unless it shows them a GAIN-then they will not buy!"
  D. Quality Customer Leads:
    1. Level of need Ability to pay
    2. Authority to pay Accessibility

3. Sympathetic attitude Business history
4. One-source buyer Reputation (price or quality buyer)

Notes and strategies for your business:

_____

_____

_____

Convert Features Into Benefits-

THE "...WHICH MEANS..." TRANSITION

FEATURES "WHICH MEANS" BENEFITS

FEATURES	BENEFITS
Performance	Time Saved
Reputation	Reduced Cost
Components	Prestige
Colors	Bigger Savings
Sizes	Greater Profits
Exclusive	Greater Convenience
Uses	Uniform Production
Applications	Uniform Accuracy
Ruggedness	Continuous Output
Delivery	Leadership
Service	Increased Sales
Price	Economy of Use
Design	Ease of Use
Availability	Reduced Inventory
Installation	Low Operating Cost
Promotion	Simplicity
Lab Tests	Reduced Upkeep
Terms	Reduced Waste
Workmanship	Long Life

BUYING MOTIVES

RATIONAL	EMOTIONAL
Economy of Purchase	Pride of Appearance
Economy of Use	Pride of Ownership
Efficient Profits	Desire of Prestige
Increased Profits	Desire for Recognition
Durability	Desire to Imitate
Accurate Performance	Desire for Variety

Labor-Saving Safety
Simple Construction
Simple Operation
Ease of Repair
Ease of Installation

Time-Saving Fear
Desire to Create
Desire for Security
Convenience
Desire to Be Unique

- Space-Saving Curiosity
- Increased Production
- Availability
- Complete Servicing
- Good Workmanship
- Low Maintenance
- Thorough Research
- Desire to be Unique
- Curiosity

Price / Quality Matrix

SALES APPEALS

	High Price	Medium Price	Low Price
High Quality	"Rolls Royce"	"We Try Harder"	"Best Buy"
Medium Quality	"Out Performs"	"Piece of the Rock"	"Smart Shopper"
Low Quality	"Feature Packed"	"Keeps on Ticking"	Bargain Hunter"

Appendix 2

Financial Management

1. Income Projection Statement
2. Balance Sheet
3. Monthly Cash Flow Projection
4. Information Resources

Income Projection Statement

Industry	J F M A M J J A S O N D	Annual	Annual %	Total %
Total net sales (revenues)				
Costs of sales				
Gross profit				
Gross profit margin				

Controllable expenses

Salaries/wages _____

Payroll expenses _____

Legal/accounting _____

Advertising _____

Automobile _____

Office supplies _____

Dues/Subscriptions _____

Utilities _____

Miscellaneous _____

Total controllable _____

Expenses

Fixed expenses _____

Rent _____

Depreciation _____

Utilities _____

Insurance _____

License/permits _____

Loan payments _____

Miscellaneous _____

Total fixed expenses _____

Total expenses _____

Net profit (loss) _____

Before taxes _____

Taxes_____

Net profit (loss) after taxes _____

Instructions For Income Projections Statement

The income projections (profit and loss) statement is valuable as both a planning tool and a key management tool to help control business operations. It enables the owner/manager to develop a preview of the amount of income generated each month and for the business year, based on reasonable predictions of monthly levels of sales, costs and expenses.

As monthly projections are developed and entered into the income projections statement, they can serve as definite goals for controlling the business operation. As actual operating results become known each month, they should be recorded for comparison with the monthly projections. A completed income statement allows the owner/manager to compare actual figures with monthly projections and to take steps to correct any problems.

CHAPTER 3: *THE BUSINESS PLAN - ROAD MAP TO SUCCESS*

Industry Percentage
In the industry percentage column, enter the percentages of total sales (revenues) that are standard for your industry, which are derived by dividing costs/expenses items x 100%

_____ total net sales

These percentages can be obtained from various sources, such as trade associations, accountants or banks. The reference librarian in your nearest public library can refer you to documents that contain the percentage figures, for example, Robert Morris Associates' Annual Statement Studies (One Liberty Place, Philadelphia, PA 19103).

Industry figures serve as a useful bench mark against which to compare cost and expense estimates that you develop for your firm. Compare the figures in the industry percentage column to those in the annual percentage column.

Total Net Sales (Revenues)
Determine the total number of units of products or services you realistically expect to sell each month in each department at the prices you expect to get. Use this step to create the projections to review your pricing practices.

• What returns, allowances and markdowns can be expected?

• Exclude any revenue that is not strictly related to the business.

Cost of Sales
The key to calculating your cost of sales is that you do not overlook any costs that you have incurred. Calculate cost of sales of all products and services used to determine total net sales. Where inventory is involved, do not overlook transportation costs. Also include any direct labor.

Gross Profit
Subtract the total cost of sales from the total net sales to obtain gross profit.

Gross Profit Margin
The gross profit is expressed as a percentage of total sales (revenues). It is calculated by dividing gross profits

_____ total net sales

Controllable (also known as Variable) Expenses
• Salary expenses-Base pay plus overtime.
• Payroll expenses-Include paid vacations, sick leave, health insurance, unemployment insurance and social security taxes.
• Outside services-Include costs of subcontracts, overflow work and special or one-time services.
• Supplies-Services and items purchased for use in the business.
• Repair and maintenance-Regular maintenance and repair, including periodic large expenditures such as painting.
• Advertising-Include desired sales volume and classified directory advertising expenses.
• Car delivery and travel-Include charges if personal car is used in business, including parking, tools, buying trips, etc.
• Accounting and legal-Outside professional services.

Fixed Expenses
• Rent-List only real estate used in business.
• Depreciation-Amortization of capital assets.
• Utilities-Water, heat, light, etc.
• Insurance-Fire or liability on property or products.
• Include workers' compensation.
• Loan repayments-Interest on outstanding loans.
• Miscellaneous-Unspecified; small expenditures without separate accounts.

Net Profit (loss)
(before taxes) - Subtract total expenses from gross profit. Taxes - Include inventory and sales tax, excise tax, real estate tax, etc.

Net Profit (loss)
(after taxes) - Subtract taxes from net profit (before taxes)

Annual Total - For each of the sales and expense items in your income projection statement, add all the monthly figures across the table and put the result in the annual total column.

Annual Percentage - Calculate the annual percentage by dividing Annual total x 100%

_____ total net sales

• Compare this figure to the industry percentage in the first column.

Balance Sheet

COMPANY NAME

As of _____, 20____

Assets

- Current assets
  Cash $_____
  Petty cash $_____
  Accounts receivable $_____
  Inventory $_____
  Short-term investment $_____
  Prepaid expenses $_____
  Long-term investment $_____

- Fixed assets
  Land $_____
  Buildings $_____
  Improvements $_____
  Equipment $_____
  Furniture $_____
  Automobile/vehicles $_____
  Other assets
      1. $_____
      2. $_____
      3. $_____
      4. $_____

- Total assets $_____

Liabilities

- Current Liabilities
  Accounts payable $_____
  Notes payable $_____
  Interest payable $_____

- Taxes payable
  Federal income tax $_____
  State income tax $_____

Self-employment tax $_____
Sales tax (SBE) $_____
Property tax $_____
Payroll accrual $_____

- Long-term liabilities
    Notes payable $_____

Total liabilities $_____
Net worth (owner equity) $_____

Proprietorship or Partnership
(name's) equity $_____
(name's) equity $_____
or Corporation
Capital stock $_____
Surplus paid in $_____
Retained earnings $_____
Total net worth $_____

- Total liabilities and total net worth $_____

(Total assets will always equal total liabilities and total net worth)

Instructions For Balance Sheet

Figures used to compile the balance sheet are taken from the previous and current balance sheet as well as the current income statement. The income statement is usually attached to the balance sheet. The following text covers the essential elements of the balance sheet.

At the top of the page fill in the legal name of the business, the type of statement and the day, month and year.

Assets
List anything of value that is owned or legally due the business. Total assets include all net values. These are the amounts derived when you subtract depreciation and amortization from the original costs of acquiring the assets.

CHAPTER 3: *THE BUSINESS PLAN - ROAD MAP TO SUCCESS*

Current Assets

- Cash-List cash and resources that can be converted into cash within 12 months of the date of the balance sheet (or during one established cycle of operation). Include money on hand and demand deposits in the bank, e.g., checking accounts and regular savings accounts.

- Petty cash-If your business has a fund for small miscellaneous expenditures, include the total here.

- Accounts receivable-The amounts due from customers in payment for merchandise or services.

- Inventory-Includes raw materials on hand, work in progress and all finished goods, either manufactured or purchased for resale.

- Short-term investments-Also called temporary investments or marketable securities, these include interest- or dividend-yielding holdings expected to be converted into cash within a year. List stocks and bonds, certificates of deposit and time-deposit savings accounts at either their cost or market value, whichever is less.

- Prepaid expenses-Goods, benefits or services a business buys or rents in advance. Examples are office supplies, insurance protection and floor space.

Long-term Investments

Also called long-term assets, these are holdings the business intends to keep for at least a year and that typically yield interest or dividends. Included are stocks, bonds and savings accounts earmarked for special purposes.

Fixed Assets

Also called plant and equipment. Includes all resources a business owns or acquires for use in operations and not intended for resale. Fixed assets may be leased. Depending on the leasing arrangements, both the value and the liability of the leased property may need to be listed on the balance sheet.

- Land-List original purchase price without allowances for market value.

- Buildings

- Improvements

- Equipment

- Furniture

- Automobile/vehicles

Liabilities

Current Liabilities

List all debts, monetary obligations and claims payable within 12 months or within one cycle of operation. Typically they include the following:

- Accounts payable-Amounts owed to suppliers for goods and services purchased in connection with business operations.

- Notes payable-The balance of principal due to pay off short-term debt for borrowed funds. Also includes the current amount due of total balance on notes whose terms exceed 12 months.

- Interest payable-Any accrued fees due for use of both short- and long-term borrowed capital and credit extended to the business.

- Taxes payable-Amounts estimated by an accountant to have been incurred during the accounting period.

- Payroll accrual-Salaries and wages currently owed.

Long-term Liabilities

Notes payable-List notes, contract payments or mortgage payments due over a period exceeding 12 months or one cycle of operation. They are listed by outstanding balance less the current position due.

Net worth

Also called owner's equity, net worth is the claim of the owner(s) on the assets of the business. In a proprietorship or partnership, equity is each owner's original investment plus any earnings after withdrawals.

Total Liabilities and Net Worth

The sum of these two amounts must always match that for total assets.

Monthly Cash Flow Projection

Name of Business Owner

Type of Business

Prepared by

Date

Pre-start- 1 2 3 4 5 6 Total

up position Columns 1-6

Year Month

Est.* Act.* Est.Act. Est.Act. Est.Act. Est.Act. Est.Act. Est.Act. Est.Act.

1. Cash on hand (beginning month)
2. Cash receipts
    (a) Cash sales
    (b) Collections from credit accounts
    (c) Loan or other cash injections (specify)
3. Total cash receipts
    (2a+2b+2c=3)
4. Total cash available
    (before cash out) (1+3)
5. Cash paid out
    (a) purchases (merchandise)
    (b) Gross wages (excludes withdrawals)
    (c) Payroll expenses (taxes, etc.)
    (d) Outside services
    (e) Supplies (office and operating)
    (f) Repairs and maintenance
    (g) Advertising
    (h) Car, delivery and travel
    (i) Accounting and legal
    (j) Rent
    (k) Telephone
    (l) Utilities
    (m) Insurance
    (n) Taxes (real estate, etc.)
    (o) Interest
    (p) Other expenses (specify each)
    (q) Miscellaneous (unspecified)
    (r) Subtotal
    (s) Loan principal payment

(t) Capital purchases (specify)
(u) Other start-up costs
(v) Reserve and/or escrow (specify)
(w) Owner's withdrawal

6. Total cash paid out (5a through 5w)
7. Cash position (end of month) (4 minus 6)
   Essential operating data (non-cash flow information)
   A. Sales volume (dollars)
   B. Accounts receivable (end on month)
   C. Bad debt (end of month)
   D. Inventory on hand (end of month)
   E. Accounts payable (end of month)

Instructions For Monthly Cash Flow Projection

1. Cash on hand (beginning of month) -- Cash on hand same as (7),

• Cash position, pervious month

2. Cash receipts-

   (a) Cash sales-All cash sales. Omit credit sales unless cash is actually received

   (b) Gross wages (including withdrawals)-- Amount to be expected from all accounts.

   (c) Loan or other cash injection-Indicate here all cash injections not shown in 2(a) or 2(b) above.

3. Total cash receipts (2a+2b+2c=3)

4. Total cash available (before cash out)(1+3)

5. Cash paid out -

   (a) Purchases (merchandise)--Merchandise for resale or for use in product (paid for in current month).

   (b) Gross wages (including withdrawals)--Base pay plus overtime (if any)

CHAPTER 3: *THE BUSINESS PLAN - ROAD MAP TO SUCCESS*

(c) Payroll expenses (taxes, etc.)-- Include paid vacations, paid sick leave, health insurance, unemployment insurance, (this might be 10 to 45% of 5(b))

(d) Outside services-This could include outside labor and/or material for specialized or overflow work, including subcontracting

(e) Supplies (office and operating)--Items purchased for use in the business (not for resale)

(f) Repairs and maintenance-Include periodic large expenditures such as painting or decorating

(g) Advertising-This amount should be adequate to maintain sales volume

(h) Car, delivery and travel-If personal car is used, charge in this column, include parking

(i) Accounting and legal-Outside services, including, for example, bookkeeping

(j) Rent-Real estate only (See 5(p) for other rentals)

(k) Telephone

(l) Utilities-Water, heat, light and/or power

(m) Insurance-Coverage on business property and products (fire, liability); also worker's compensation, fidelity, etc. Exclude executive life (include in 5(w))

(n) Taxes (real estate, etc.)-- Plus inventory tax, sales tax, excise tax, if applicable

(o) Interest-Remember to add interest on loan as it is injected (See 2© above)

(p) Other expenses (specify each)
 • Unexpected expenditures may be included here as a safety factor
 • Equipment expenses during the month should be included here (non-capital equipment)
 • When equipment is rented or leased, record payments here

(q) Miscellaneous (unspecified)--Small expenditures for which separate accounts would be practical

(r) Subtotal-This subtotal indicates cash out for operating costs

(s) Loan principal payment-Include payment on all loans, including vehicle and equipment purchases on time payment

(t) Capital purchases (specify)--Nonexpensed (depreciable) expenditures such as equipment, building purchases on time payment

(u) Other start-up costs-Expenses incurred prior to first month projection and paid for after start-up

(v) Reserve and/or escrow (specify)-- Example: insurance, tax or equipment escrow to reduce impact of large periodic payments

(w) Owner's withdrawals-Should include payment for such things as owner's income tax, social security, health insurance, executive life insurance premiums, etc.

6. Total cash paid out (5a through 5w)

7. Cash position (end on month) (4 minus 6)-- Enter this amount in (1) Cash on hand following month-
Essential operating data (non-cash flow information)--This is basic information necessary for proper planning and for proper cash flow projection. Also with this data, the cash flow can be evolved and shown in the above form.

A. Sales volume (dollars)--This is a very important figure and should be estimated carefully, taking into account size of facility and employee output as well as realistic anticipated sales (actual sales, not orders received).

B. Accounts receivable (end of month)-- Previous unpaid credit sales plus current month's credit sales, less amounts received current month (deduct "C" below)

C. Bad debt (end on month)-- Bad debts should be subtracted from (B) in the month anticipated

D. Inventory on hand (end on month)-- Last month's inventory plus merchandise received and/or manufactured current month minus amount sold current month

E. Accounts payable (end of month) Previous month's payable plus current month's payable minus amount paid during month.

CHAPTER 3: *THE BUSINESS PLAN - ROAD MAP TO SUCCESS*

F. Depreciation-Established by your accountant, or value of all your equipment divided by useful life (in months) as allowed by Internal Revenue Service

Appendix 3: Information Resources

U.S. Small Business Administration (SBA)

The SBA offers an extensive selection of information on most business management topics, from how to start a business to exporting your products.

This information is listed in "Resource Directory for Small Business Management." For a free copy contact your nearest SBA office.

SBA has offices throughout the country. Consult the U.S. Government section in your telephone directory for the office nearest you. SBA offers a number of programs and services, including training and educational programs, counseling services, financial programs and contract assistance. Ask about

- Service Corps of Retired Executives (SCORE), a national organization sponsored by SBA of over 13,000 volunteer business executives who provide free counseling, workshops and seminars to prospective and existing small business people.

- Small Business Development Centers (SBDCs), sponsored by the SBA in partnership with state and local governments, the educational community and the private sector. They provide assistance, counseling and training to prospective and existing business people.

- Business Information Centers (BICs), offering state-of-the-art technology, informational resources and on-site counseling for start-up and expanding businesses to create business, marketing and other plans, do research, and receive expert training and assistance.

For more information about SBA business development programs and services, call the SBA Small Business Answer Desk at 1-800-U-ASK-SBA (827-5722).

Other U.S. Government Resources

Many publications on business management and other related topics are available from the Government Printing Office (GPO). GPO bookstores are located in 24 major cities and listed in the Yellow Pages under the "bookstore" heading. You can request a "Subject Bibliography" by writing to Government Printing Office, Superintendent of Documents, Washington, DC 20402-9328.

Many federal agencies offer publications of interest to small businesses. There is a nominal fee for some, but most are free. Below is a selected list of government agencies that provide publications and other services targeted to small businesses. To get their publications, contract the regional offices listed in the telephone directory or write to the addresses below:

- Consumer Information Center (CIC)
  P.O. Box 100
  Pueblo, CO 81002
  The CIC offers a consumer information catalog of federal publications.

- Consumer Product Safety Commission (CPSC)
  Publications Request
  Washington, DC 20207
  The CPSC offers guidelines for product safety requirements.

- U.S. Department of Agriculture (USDA)
  12th Street and Independence Avenue, SW
  Washington, DC 20250
  The USDA offers publications on selling to the USDA. Publications and programs on entrepreneurship are also available through county extension offices nationwide.

- U.S. Department of Commerce (DOC)
  Office of Business Liaison
  14th Street and Constitution Avenue, NW
  Room 5898C
  Washington, DC 20230
  DOC's Business Assistance Center provides listings of business opportunities available in the federal government. This service also will refer businesses to different programs and services in the DOC and other federal agencies.

- U.S. Department of Health and Human Services (HHS) - Public
  Health Service
  Alcohol, Drug Abuse and Mental Health Administration
  5600 Fishers Lane
  Rockville, MD 20857
  Drug Free Workplace Helpline: 1-800-843-4971. Provides information on Employee Assistance Programs.

CHAPTER 3: *THE BUSINESS PLAN - ROAD MAP TO SUCCESS*

National Institute for Drug Abuse Hotline:
1-800-662-4357. Provides information on preventing substance abuse in the workplace.

The National Clearinghouse for Alcohol and Drug Information:
1-800-729-6686 toll-free. Provides pamphlets and resource materials on substance abuse.

- U.S. Department of Labor (DOL)
  Employment Standards Administration
  200 Constitution Avenue, NW
  Washington, DC 20210
  The DOL offers publications on compliance with labor laws.

- U.S. Department of Treasury
  Internal Revenue Service (IRS)
  P.O. Box 25866
  Richmond, VA 23260
  1-800-424-3676
  The IRS offers information on tax requirements for small businesses.

- Environmental Protection Agency Office of Small Business Ombudsman
  U.S. Environmental Protection Agency (EPA)
  Small Business Ombudsman (Mail Code 2131)
  Room 3423
  401 M Street, S.W.
  Washington, D.C. 20460
  1-800-368-5888 except in DC and VA
  202-260-1211 in DC and VA
  The EPA offers more than 100 publications designed to help small businesses understand how they can comply with EPA regulations.

- U.S. Food and Drug Administration (FDA)
  FDA Center for Food Safety and Applied Nutrition
  200 C Street, SW
  Washington, DC 20204
  The FDA offers information on packaging and labeling requirements for food and food-related products.

For More Information

A librarian can help you locate the specific information you need in reference books. Most libraries have a variety of directories, indexes and encyclopedias that cover many business topics. They also have other resources, such as

- Trade association information

- Ask the librarian to show you a directory of trade associations. Associations provide a valuable network of resources to their members through publications and services such as newsletters, conferences and seminars.

Books
Many guidebooks, textbooks and manuals on small business are published annually. To find the names of books not in your local library check Books In Prints, a directory of books currently available from publishers.

Magazine and newspaper articles
Business and professional magazines provide information that is more current than that found in books and textbooks. There are a number of indexes to help you find specific articles in periodicals.

In addition to books and magazines, many libraries offer free workshops, lend skill-building tapes and have catalogues and brochures describing continuing education opportunities.

Source: U.S. Small Business Administration (used with permission)

Chapter 4: Getting Started

A home-based collection agency has many advantages. The ability to keep your overhead low and minimal start-up costs are the most obvious benefits.

Lets talk about what you need to get started:

Computer: A new computer, sufficient to meet your immediate needs, can be purchased for approximately $650.00. Basic spreadsheet and word processing software is standard on most computers.

Printer: I am looking at a Staples flyer right now advertising an all-in-one Lexmark color printer, copier, fax and scanner for $179.98. I have seen even lower prices.

Business Cards: I purchased 250 business cards from VistaPrint.com for "free" paying only the shipping cost of about $5.95.

High Quality Marketing Postcards: My initial 250 custom order cost $49.99.

Imprinted Pens: I ordered 500 imprinted pens from Pens.com for $87.50. The cost broke down to 250 pens @ .35 ea. Plus 250 "free" pens. Those stick pens actually write real nice.

Initial postage and misc. expenses: $350.

Collection Software: I purchased Abacus Totality Collection Software for Windows. I found it affordable and easy to use. Cost: $500. This is optional until you have a client base and start making money.

Lets round-off our numbers and sub-total:
$650   Computer (if you don't have one)
$180   All-in-one fax etc.
$6   Business cards
$50   Postcards
$90   Pens
$350   Initial postage & misc.
$500   Optional collection software – if you can afford it.
$1826   **Total** (does not include bonding/license expenses, if required by law)

If a computer doesn't need to be purchased and you manually track clients on a spreadsheet until you can afford the collection software, the sub-total drops to only $676.00.

Before we arrive at a grand total – lets talk business name and web site.

Note: I did not bother discussing the need for a chair, desk, file cabinet etc. Most people have a desk and chair and you can use hanging folders in an open storage box, if you can't afford a file cabinet yet.

Chapter 5: Your Business and Domain Name

Your Business Name is Critical

Your business and domain name should give someone a general idea of what services you offer. It should be easy to remember.

For example, I just thought of a domain name: Debt2Profit.com and checked on its availability. It was not registered. But it is now. I just bought it.

In my opinion Debt2Profit is an easy to remember name and gives a clear picture of what a collection agency hopes to do for clients.

GoDaddy.com

A great place to buy domain names is GoDaddy.com. GoDaddy offers domain names as low as $8.95, transfers for $7.75, hosting for under $10.00 and you can cancel at anytime.

Note: With all this talk of the internet, don't forget to check with the county clerks office or other applicable authorities in your area to determine what business license(s) or other documents you may need to run an agency out of your home.

Chapter 6: Your Web Site and Total Start-Up Costs

The Internet - No Reason to Wait

According to a 2002 ACA International Study 69% of all collection agencies had their own web site – and you should too.

Please understand a web site by itself is not going to drive business to your doorstep. Your web site should be an extension of all your other marketing efforts. Every piece of literature and every give away product should have your web site address prominently featured.

How much information can you put on a business card or post card? Not too much. But if these items have your web site listed, a potential client can access all the FAQ about your services at his or her leisure. They can also email questions or concerns.

When I was in the early stages of developing my web site, I tried to read all I could about search engine placement, key words, meta tags, internet directories and a zillion other related issues. It was overwhelming for someone trying to close one business, start another business and still look for a job during the day. I decided I needed assistance and sought the help of a professional web designer.

Tight Budget

The initial web site design cost was $700.00. When I added a page or significantly changed text, a billing statement would be generated for $50, $100 or more. The truth was I didn't really control my web site. I was satisfied with the end product, but it was more than a start-up collection agency on a tight budget needed.

GoDaddy.com to the Rescue

GoDaddy.com has a product called Website Design 5.0. This software comes with 420 templates and 2500 images! The initial cost: $14.95!!!!! You can host your site at GoDaddy for less than $10.00 a month and can cancel at anytime. Your total cost for the first year is under $200.00. In addition to the low cost another benefit is that you are in charge of your web site.

CHAPTER 6: *YOUR WEB SITE AND TOTAL START-UP COSTS*

Search Engine's and Directories

As for your web site placement in search engines and directories – don't drive yourself nuts. Take a small portion of the $1000.00 plus you saved in development costs and put it to work with internet marketing programs like:

Google AdWords™ that enables you to manage your own account, and with cost-per-click (CPC) pricing, you pay only when users click on your ad. You control your costs by setting a daily budget for what you are willing to spend each day.

Overture.com: When you advertise in Overture Premium Listings™, your business appears in the top U.S. search sites: MSN, Yahoo!, InfoSpace, Lycos, AltaVista, and Netscape. You set the price you're willing to pay for each sales lead and pay only when your customers click through to your site.

Grand Total

Now lets go back to those "Getting Started" sub-totals and add $200.00 to cover your web page design, hosting for the first 6 months and domain registration and add $300.00 as a little cushion.

$650	Computer (if you don't have one)
$180	All-in-one fax etc.
$6	Business cards
$50	Postcards
$90	Pens
$350	Initial postage & misc.
$500	Optional collection software – if you can afford it.
$1826	**Subtotal**
$200	Web design etc.
$300	Cushion
$2326	**Grand Total**

Already Have a Computer?

If a computer doesn't need to be purchased and you manually track clients on a spreadsheet until you can afford the collection software the sub-total drops even further:

$676	Subtotal without computer and software
$200	Web design etc.
$300	Cushion
$1176	**Grand Total**

So there you have it.

Depending upon your particular circumstances you will need approximately $1200 to $2400 to get Your Collection Agency off the ground. Again, this would not include any licensing/bonding expenses, if required by law.

Cash Is King

Be extremely careful not to waste money. Your first objective is to get a steady stream of income for your agency. You should have some other source of income during the initial start-up phase.

Always keep a financial cushion for the bad times. Most likely your income at this stage will be irregular. If you have a great month, only spend a portion toward growing your business. DO NOT spend all your cash.

Wouldn't it be awkward to acquire a new client and find out you don't have enough money for postage and other fixed expenses because you took a large salary draw or purchased non-critical office equipment too soon.

Chapter 7: Marketing Your Collection Agency

Your web site, business cards and post cards are only a small part of your overall marketing plan. You will need to broadcast your services anyway you can 24/7. Here are some additional marketing ideas:

Start a Newsletter For Your Targeted Audience.

DO NOT make yourself the focus of the newsletter. Think back. How many newsletters have you received and how many have you saved. You probably saved only a handful. Why? Because many newsletters tell us about things we are not interested in reading about.

Your newsletter should contain information of value to the recipient. Sure you can "advertise" your service and should…but be subtle. Include information that addresses the wants and needs of your prospective client. Fill it with useful information that makes the recipient want to save it.

Cold Call

Perform a self-assessment of your skill and level of comfort in this area. Many books will try to teach you tricks to reach the decision maker. Call early in the morning or after 5:00pm. Try to word your statement in a way that gets you through the secretary. I have never liked these approaches.

The Gatekeeper

My approach was to find the "gatekeeper" of the decision maker and win them over. You should:
• Use a soft approach
• Acknowledge how busy they are
• Offer to call back at a more convenient time. In fact, I prefer to have a second conversation.
• Ask permission to send some information to them…not the decision maker.
• Empower them. They are in fact a decision maker. They will decide who gets through that door to the Big Guy (or Lady).

A similar approach can be used when cold calling in person. Utilize some of the following:
• Postcards

• Pens
• Brochures

My goal was to get to see the "gatekeeper" and make it clear I didn't want to be intrusive. I presented myself as someone just dropping off some literature for the person in charge of accounts receivable collections. I was always deferential. I would always exit quickly...unless they asked questions. A week or two later I would follow-up with a letter or phone call.

Who do you think has a better shot at selling a service? The person who tricked the "gatekeeper" to get to the head honcho and only wanted 15 minutes of uninvited time or the person who came recommended by the "gatekeeper?"

Classified Ads

You can find leads in newspapers by checking out companies hiring help that requires billing & collection skills. Most likely this type business uses the service of a collection agency already.

Sales Letter

Keep it simple. Nobody will read a solid page of text in 8-point type. Many businesses will tell you of past "bad experiences" with a given collection agency. You need to explain why you are different. You want to be an extension of their office and the buck stops with you – not some inexperienced collector on a large staff. At the end of your letter, ask them to call or visit your web site for additional information.

Flyers / Brochures

When you put your brochure together, give it a professional, but not too slick look...again you are trying to look different. I submitted my project for bid to A2Zmoonlighter.com, a professional moonlighter site. I was able to smooth out the edges of my brochure and give it a professional (but not too slick) appearance for $100.00. The designer who worked on my brochure (and this book), Ben Carpenter, can be contacted through his web site at www.bc2design.com.

Publicity

Why not check out local newspapers to see if they will do a story about your business – after you are up and running.

CHAPTER 7: *MARKETING YOUR COLLECTION AGENCY*

Inserts

You will want to target businesses not consumers. My local Chamber of Commerce offers the following:

Option 1: If I provide 400 copies of my one-page flyer; they prepare the bulk mailing and provide the postage.
Cost $50

Option 2: If I provide the original one-page flyer; they copy it, prepare the bulk mailing and provide postage.
Cost $80 (one-sided), $90 (two-sided)

Perhaps your Chamber has something similar.

Chapter 8: Sample Sales Letter

Your sales letter should highlight the fact that you are the "alternative" to the big collection agency experience. Do not be ashamed of being small. Instead embrace the fact that you are small.

The following is one of many approaches you might take:

Dear Ms. Prospect:

My name is Janet Gainer. I am the owner / operator of the XYZ Collection Agency. I offer an alternative solution to the "big" collection agency experience.

As you may have experienced, large collection agencies tend to focus on large volume clients and high dollar claims. Conversely, I am in the business of helping small businesses and healthcare practices.

As the sole collector, I can assure you of consistent claims processing and follow-up. When you have a question or concern, you will speak directly with me...not one of a dozen staff collectors. My goal is to forge a "personal" long-term relationship with you and your firm.

My fee is based upon a percentage of the accounts I collect. No Collection. No Charge. The first consultation is free. I honestly believe I can increase your cash flow, reduce your overhead and manage your accounts professionally and ethically.

If you have any further questions, please do not hesitate to call.

Kind regards,

Janet

[Note: Your letterhead should list your web site and email address.]

Chapter 9: State Licensing Contacts

State Licensing Contacts:

Alabama State Of, Revenue Department, Sales Use & Business Tax Division, Severance & License, (334) 353-7827, Montgomery, AL 36104

Alaska State Of, Community & Economic Development Dept Of, Occupational Licensing Div Of, Boards Commissions & Trades, Athletic Commission, (907) 465-2695, Juneau, AK 99801

Arizona State Government, Banking Department, (602) 255-4421, 2910 N 44th St Ste 310, Phoenix, AZ 85018

Arkansas State Of, Collections State Board Of, (501) 376-9814, Little Rock, AR 72201

California State Of, Secretary of State 1500 11 th Street 916-653-7244 Sacramento, CA 95814

Colorado, Attorney General 1525 Sherman St. 7th floor Denver, CO 80203, Attn: Collection Agency Licensing (303) 866-5706 Collection Agency Board - cab@state.co.us

Connecticut Banking Commissioner 260 Constitution Plaza Hartford, CT 06103
860-240-8299   800-831-7225 (toll free in CT)

Delaware Secretary of State PO BOX 898 401 Federal St, Suite 3 Dover, DE 19903-0898 PHONE: 302-739-4111 FAX: 302-739-3811

District of Columbia, Corp. Division, Department of Consumer & Regulatory Affairs, 614 H. Street NW, Room 407, 20001 (202) 727 7278

Florida State Of, Banking & Finance Department Of, Securities Finance Division Of, Director, (850) 410-9805, Tallahassee, FL 32301

Georgia State Government, Secretary Of State, Secretary Of State, (404) 656-2881, 214 State Capitol, Atlanta, GA 30303

Hawaii State Government, Commerce & Consumer Affairs Department Of, Professional & Vocational Licensing Division, Department of Commerce and Consumer Affairs, (808) 586-2693, Honolulu, HI 96813

Idaho State Government, Finance Department Of, Administration, (208) 332-8000, 700 W State St, Boise, ID 83702

Illinois Department of Professional Regulation 320 West Washington Street, 3 rd floor. Springfield, IL 62786 (217) 782-6742

Indiana State Of, Securities Division, (317) 232-6681, 302 W Washington St Room E111, Indianapolis, IN 46204

Iowa Consumer Protection Division- Attorney General, (515) 281-5926, Hoover Bldg, Des Moines, IA 50307

Kansas Secretary of State: Ron Thornburgh, State Capitol, 2nd Fl., Topeka, KS 66612-1594

Kentucky State Of, Secretary Of State, Office Of The Secretary, (502) 564-3490, 700 Capitol Ave Frankfort, KY 40601

Louisiana Office of Financial Institutions PO Box 94095 Baton Rouge LA 70804-9095 (225) 925-4660 ofila@ofi.state.la.us

Maine State Of, Professional & Financial Regulation Dept Of, Consumer Credit Regulation, Debt Collector Licensing (207) 624-8527, Augusta, ME 04330

Maryland Commissioner of Financial Regulation (410) 230-6100, 500 North Calvert Street, Suite 402 Baltimore, MD 21202, http://www.dllr.state.md.us/license/fin_reg/colagency/colagency.htm

Massachusetts Commonwealth Of, Banks Division Of, (617) 956-1500, 20 East St, Boston, MA 02111

Michigan Department of Consumer and Industry Services Collection Practices Board PO Box 30018 Lansing, MI 48909 Tel: 517-373-1654

Minnesota Department of Commerce, 85 7th Place East, Suite 500, St. Paul, MN 55101 Licensing Division 1-800-657-3978 licensing.commerce@state.mn.us

CHAPTER 9: *STATE LICENSING CONTACTS*

Mississippi State Government, Secretary Of State, (601) 359-1350, Jackson, MS 39201

Missouri State Of, Secretary Of State Office Of, (573) 751-4936, 600 W Main St, Jefferson City, MO 65101

Montana Office of the Secretary of State Room 260, Capitol PO Box 202801 Helena, MT 59620-2801 406-444-2034 sos@state.mt.us

Nebraska Collection Agency Licensing Board, (402) 471-2555, Suite 2300 State Capitol Building Lincoln, NE 68509

Nevada Department of Business & Industry Financial Institutions Division 406 E. Second Street, Suite 3 Carson City, Nevada 89701-4758 (702) 687-4259

New Hampshire State Of, Secretary Of States Office, (603) 271-3242, State House, Concord, NH 03301

New Jersey DOR/Business Services, (609) 292-9292, PO Box 308, Trenton, NJ 08625

New Mexico State Government, Regulation and Licensing Department, Financial Institutions Division 725 St. Michael's Dr. Santa Fe, NM 87505 Phone: 505-827-7100

New York State, State Department Of, Secretary Of State, (518) 474-0050, Albany, NY 12202

Buffalo City Of, License Office, (716) 851-4951, Buffalo, NY 14201

New York City Dept. of Consumer Affairs 42 Broadway New York, NY 10004 Phone: 212-487-4444

North Carolina State Government, Insurance, Special Services, (919) 733-2200, Raleigh, NC 27601

North Dakota State Of, Banking & Financial Institutions Department Of, (701) 328-9933, 2000 Schafer St Ste G, Bismarck, ND 58501

Ohio, State of, Secretary of State, Blackwell, Kenneth, R, 30 East Broad St. 14th Floor, Columbus, OH, 43266, (614) 466-2655

Pennsylvania Commonwealth Of, State Department Of, Executive Office, 302 North Capitol

Building (717) 787-7630, Harrisburg, PA 17105

Rhode Island, Secretary of State 218, State House Providence, RI 02903 401-277-2357. http://www.state.ri.us/

South Carolina Secretary of State Edgar Brown Bldg., Ste. 525, Box 11350, Columbia,SC 29211 Telephone: (803) 734-2170

South Dakota State Of, Capitol Building & Associated Offices, Secretary Of State, (605) 773-3537, Pierre, SD 57501

Tennessee Collection Service Board Davy Crockett Tower 500 James Robertson Parkway, 6th Floor Nashville, Tennessee 37243 Phone (615) 741-1741

Texas State Of, Secretary Of State, Statutory Filings Division, Statutory Documents Section, Health Spas, (512) 463-6906, Austin, TX 78701

Utah Department of Commerce S.M. Box 146705, 160 East 300 South, 1st Floor, Salt Lake City, UT 84114-6705 Corporation's Information Center: (801)530-4849. Collection Agency Registration. The application must be typewritten or computer generated, if it is handwritten it will be returned. Requests for applications must be made in writing or by faxing your request to (801) 530-6438. You may also e-mail your request to orders@br.state.ut.us

Vermont, Secretary of State, 109 State St. Montpelier, VT 05609-1101. Phone: (802) 828-2148

Virginia Commonwealth Of, Commonwealth Secretary Of The, (804) 786-2441, Richmond, VA 23219

Washington State Of, Licenses & Certifications, Collection Agency Licenses, (360) 664-1389, Olympia, WA 98501

West Virginia Department of Tax and Revenue, Revenue Center, 1001 Lee Street, East PO Box 2389, Charleston, West Virginia 25328-2389, (304) 558-8500

Wisconsin Department of Financial Institutions, 345 W Washington Avenue, Madison, WI 53703, (608) 261-9555

Wyoming State Government, Audit Department, Collection Agency Board, (307) 777-3497, Cheyenne, WY 82009. http://audit.state.wy.us/banking/cab/cabapplicationforms.htm

CHAPTER 9: *STATE LICENSING CONTACTS*

Disclaimer: The material in this book is not intended to be, and is not a substitute for, professional legal materials or counsel. Reasonable efforts have been made to include accurate and up-to-date information. You should not rely on the information and materials contained in this book for any purposes except as a general guide to starting a collection agency. You are responsible for seeking verification from professional legal materials and consulting independent legal counsel.

Chapter 10: The Fair Debt Collection Practices Act

The FAIR DEBT COLLECTION PRACTICES ACT (FDCPA) applies to debt collectors attempting to collect "consumer" debts. Business debts are not covered by the FDCPA, but it is still wise to act in an ethical and professional manner in all debt collection situations.

Here is a small sample of "DON'T" items:

DON'T:

- Call a consumer at inconvenient times or places. That means, generally, before 8:00 a.m. or after 9:00 p.m.

- Discuss a consumers credit problems with their family members or friends. However, you may call family members and friends to try to locate a consumer.

- Continue to contact a consumer if he or she has a lawyer. You must contact the lawyer.

- If a consumer writes and tells you not to contact them again, you may only contact them one more time to let them know what legal or other action you plan to take.

- Use obscene language

- Make false statements about who you are

- Imply you are an attorney or make any other misrepresentation.

You should read and understand the entire FAIR DEBT COLLECTION PRACTICES ACT that follows:

As amended by Public Law 104-208, 110 Stat. 3009 (Sept. 30, 1996)

CHAPTER 10: *THE FAIR DEBT COLLECTION PRACTICES ACT*

To amend the Consumer Credit Protection Act to prohibit abusive practices by debt collectors.

Be it enacted by the Senate and House of Representatives of the United States of America in Congress assembled, That the Consumer Credit Protection Act (15 U.S.C. 1601 et seq.) is amended by adding at the end thereof the following new title:

TITLE VIII - DEBT COLLECTION PRACTICES [Fair Debt Collection Practices Act]

Sec.
801. Short Title
802. Congressional findings and declaration of purpose
803. Definitions
804. Acquisition of location information
805. Communication in connection with debt collection
806. Harassment or abuse
807. False or misleading representations
808. Unfair practice
809. Validation of debts
810. Multiple debts
811. Legal actions by debt collectors
812. Furnishing certain deceptive forms
813. Civil liability
814. Administrative enforcement
815. Reports to Congress by the Commission
816. Relation to State laws
817. Exemption for State regulation
818. Effective date

§ 801. Short Title [15 USC 1601 note]

This title may be cited as the "Fair Debt Collection Practices Act."

§ 802. Congressional findings and declarations of purpose [15 USC 1692]

(a) There is abundant evidence of the use of abusive, deceptive, and unfair debt collection practices by many debt collectors. Abusive debt collection practices contribute to the number of personal bankruptcies, to marital instability, to the loss of jobs, and to invasions of individual privacy.

(b) Existing laws and procedures for redressing these injuries are inadequate to protect consumers.

(c) Means other than misrepresentation or other abusive debt collection practices are available for the effective collection of debts.

(d) Abusive debt collection practices are carried on to a substantial extent in interstate commerce and through means and instrumentalities of such commerce. Even where abusive debt collection practices are purely intrastate in character, they nevertheless directly affect interstate commerce.

(e) It is the purpose of this title to eliminate abusive debt collection practices by debt collectors, to insure that those debt collectors who refrain from using abusive debt collection practices are not competitively disadvantaged, and to promote consistent State action to protect consumers against debt collection abuses.

§ 803. Definitions [15 USC 1692a]

As used in this title --

(1) The term "Commission" means the Federal Trade Commission.

(2) The term "communication" means the conveying of information regarding a debt directly or indirectly to any person through any medium.

(3) The term "consumer" means any natural person obligated or allegedly obligated to pay any debt.

(4) The term "creditor" means any person who offers or extends credit creating a debt or to whom a debt is owed, but such term does not include any person to the extent that he receives an assignment or transfer of a debt in default solely for the purpose of facilitating collection of such debt for another.

(5) The term "debt" means any obligation or alleged obligation of a consumer to pay money arising out of a transaction in which the money, property, insurance or services which are the subject of the transaction are primarily for personal, family, or household purposes, whether or not such obligation has been reduced to judgment.

CHAPTER 10: *THE FAIR DEBT COLLECTION PRACTICES ACT*

(6) The term "debt collector" means any person who uses any instrumentality of interstate commerce or the mails in any business the principal purpose of which is the collection of any debts, or who regularly collects or attempts to collect, directly or indirectly, debts owed or due or asserted to be owed or due another. Notwithstanding the exclusion provided by clause (F) of the last sentence of this paragraph, the term includes any creditor who, in the process of collecting his own debts, uses any name other than his own which would indicate that a third person is collecting or attempting to collect such debts. For the purpose of section 808(6), such term also includes any person who uses any instrumentality of interstate commerce or the mails in any business the principal purpose of which is the enforcement of security interests. The term does not include --

(A) any officer or employee of a creditor while, in the name of the creditor, collecting debts for such creditor;

(B) any person while acting as a debt collector for another person, both of whom are related by common ownership or affiliated by corporate control, if the person acting as a debt collector does so only for persons to whom it is so related or affiliated and if the principal business of such person is not the collection of debts;

(C) any officer or employee of the United States or any State to the extent that collecting or attempting to collect any debt is in the performance of his official duties;

(D) any person while serving or attempting to serve legal process on any other person in connection with the judicial enforcement of any debt;

(E) any nonprofit organization which, at the request of consumers, performs bona fide consumer credit counseling and assists consumers in the liquidation of their debts by receiving payments from such consumers and distributing such amounts to creditors; and

(F) any person collecting or attempting to collect any debt owed or due or asserted to be owed or due another to the extent such activity (i) is incidental to a bona fide fiduciary obligation or a bona fide escrow arrangement; (ii) concerns a debt which was originated by such person; (iii) concerns a debt which was not in default at the time it was obtained by such person; or (iv) concerns a debt obtained by such person as a secured party in a commercial credit transaction involving the creditor.

(7) The term "location information" means a consumer's place of abode and his telephone number at such place, or his place of employment.

(8) The term "State" means any State, territory, or possession of the United States, the District of

Columbia, the Commonwealth of Puerto Rico, or any political subdivision of any of the foregoing.

§ 804. Acquisition of location information [15 USC 1692b]

Any debt collector communicating with any person other than the consumer for the purpose of acquiring location information about the consumer shall --

(1) identify himself, state that he is confirming or correcting location information concerning the consumer, and, only if expressly requested, identify his employer;

(2) not state that such consumer owes any debt;

(3) not communicate with any such person more than once unless requested to do so by such person or unless the debt collector reasonably believes that the earlier response of such person is erroneous or incomplete and that such person now has correct or complete location information;

(4) not communicate by post card;

(5) not use any language or symbol on any envelope or in the contents of any communication effected by the mails or telegram that indicates that the debt collector is in the debt collection business or that the communication relates to the collection of a debt; and

(6) after the debt collector knows the consumer is represented by an attorney with regard to the subject debt and has knowledge of, or can readily ascertain, such attorney's name and address, not communicate with any person other than that attorney, unless the attorney fails to respond within a reasonable period of time to the communication from the debt collector.

§ 805. Communication in connection with debt collection [15 USC 1692c]

(a) COMMUNICATION WITH THE CONSUMER GENERALLY. Without the prior consent of the consumer given directly to the debt collector or the express permission of a court of competent jurisdiction, a debt collector may not communicate with a consumer in connection with the collection of any debt --

(1) at any unusual time or place or a time or place known or which should be known to be inconvenient to the consumer. In the absence of knowledge of circumstances to the contrary, a debt collector shall assume that the convenient time for communicating with a consumer is after 8 o'clock

CHAPTER 10: *THE FAIR DEBT COLLECTION PRACTICES ACT*

antimeridian and before 9 o'clock postmeridian, local time at the consumer's location;

(2) if the debt collector knows the consumer is represented by an attorney with respect to such debt and has knowledge of, or can readily ascertain, such attorney's name and address, unless the attorney fails to respond within a reasonable period of time to a communication from the debt collector or unless the attorney consents to direct communication with the consumer; or

(3) at the consumer's place of employment if the debt collector knows or has reason to know that the consumer's employer prohibits the consumer from receiving such communication.

(b) COMMUNICATION WITH THIRD PARTIES. Except as provided in section 804, without the prior consent of the consumer given directly to the debt collector, or the express permission of a court of competent jurisdiction, or as reasonably necessary to effectuate a postjudgment judicial remedy, a debt collector may not communicate, in connection with the collection of any debt, with any person other than a consumer, his attorney, a consumer reporting agency if otherwise permitted by law, the creditor, the attorney of the creditor, or the attorney of the debt collector.

(c) CEASING COMMUNICATION. If a consumer notifies a debt collector in writing that the consumer refuses to pay a debt or that the consumer wishes the debt collector to cease further communication with the consumer, the debt collector shall not communicate further with the consumer with respect to such debt, except --

(1) to advise the consumer that the debt collector's further efforts are being terminated;

(2) to notify the consumer that the debt collector or creditor may invoke specified remedies which are ordinarily invoked by such debt collector or creditor; or

(3) where applicable, to notify the consumer that the debt collector or creditor intends to invoke a specified remedy.

If such notice from the consumer is made by mail, notification shall be complete upon receipt.

(d) For the purpose of this section, the term "consumer" includes the consumer's spouse, parent (if the consumer is a minor), guardian, executor, or administrator.

§ 806. Harassment or abuse [15 USC 1692d]

A debt collector may not engage in any conduct the natural consequence of which is to harass, oppress, or abuse any person in connection with the collection of a debt. Without limiting the general application of the foregoing, the following conduct is a violation of this section:

(1) The use or threat of use of violence or other criminal means to harm the physical person, reputation, or property of any person.

(2) The use of obscene or profane language or language the natural consequence of which is to abuse the hearer or reader.

(3) The publication of a list of consumers who allegedly refuse to pay debts, except to a consumer reporting agency or to persons meeting the requirements of section 603(f) or 604(3)1 of this Act.

(4) The advertisement for sale of any debt to coerce payment of the debt.

(5) Causing a telephone to ring or engaging any person in telephone conversation repeatedly or continuously with intent to annoy, abuse, or harass any person at the called number.

(6) Except as provided in section 804, the placement of telephone calls without meaningful disclosure of the caller's identity.

§ 807. False or misleading representations [15 USC 1962e]

A debt collector may not use any false, deceptive, or misleading representation or means in connection with the collection of any debt. Without limiting the general application of the foregoing, the following conduct is a violation of this section:

(1) The false representation or implication that the debt collector is vouched for, bonded by, or affiliated with the United States or any State, including the use of any badge, uniform, or facsimile thereof.

(2) The false representation of --

(A) the character, amount, or legal status of any debt; or

(B) any services rendered or compensation which may be lawfully received by any debt collector for the collection of a debt.

(3) The false representation or implication that any individual is an attorney or that any communication is from an attorney.

(4) The representation or implication that nonpayment of any debt will result in the arrest or imprisonment of any person or the seizure, garnishment, attachment, or sale of any property or wages of any person unless such action is lawful and the debt collector or creditor intends to take such action.

(5) The threat to take any action that cannot legally be taken or that is not intended to be taken.

(6) The false representation or implication that a sale, referral, or other transfer of any interest in a debt shall cause the consumer to --

(A) lose any claim or defense to payment of the debt; or

(B) become subject to any practice prohibited by this title.

(7) The false representation or implication that the consumer committed any crime or other conduct in order to disgrace the consumer.

(8) Communicating or threatening to communicate to any person credit information which is known or which should be known to be false, including the failure to communicate that a disputed debt is disputed.

(9) The use or distribution of any written communication which simulates or is falsely represented to be a document authorized, issued, or approved by any court, official, or agency of the United States or any State, or which creates a false impression as to its source, authorization, or approval.

(10) The use of any false representation or deceptive means to collect or attempt to collect any debt or to obtain information concerning a consumer.

(11) The failure to disclose in the initial written communication with the consumer and, in addition, if the initial communication with the consumer is oral, in that initial oral communication, that the debt collector is attempting to collect a debt and that any information obtained will be used for that purpose, and the failure to disclose in subsequent communications that the communication is from a debt collector, except that this paragraph shall not apply to a formal pleading made in connection with a legal action.

(12) The false representation or implication that accounts have been turned over to innocent purchasers for value.

(13) The false representation or implication that documents are legal process.

(14) The use of any business, company, or organization name other than the true name of the debt collector's business, company, or organization.

(15) The false representation or implication that documents are not legal process forms or do not require action by the consumer.

(16) The false representation or implication that a debt collector operates or is employed by a consumer reporting agency as defined by section 603(f) of this Act.

§ 808. Unfair practices [15 USC 1692f]

A debt collector may not use unfair or unconscionable means to collect or attempt to collect any debt. Without limiting the general application of the foregoing, the following conduct is a violation of this section:

(1) The collection of any amount (including any interest, fee, charge, or expense incidental to the principal obligation) unless such amount is expressly authorized by the agreement creating the debt or permitted by law.

(2) The acceptance by a debt collector from any person of a check or other payment instrument postdated by more than five days unless such person is notified in writing of the debt collector's intent to deposit such check or instrument not more than ten nor less than three business days prior to such deposit.

(3) The solicitation by a debt collector of any postdated check or other postdated payment instrument for the purpose of threatening or instituting criminal prosecution.

(4) Depositing or threatening to deposit any postdated check or other postdated payment instrument prior to the date on such check or instrument.

(5) Causing charges to be made to any person for communications by concealment of the true propose of the communication. Such charges include, but are not limited to, collect telephone calls and telegram fees.

(6) Taking or threatening to take any nonjudicial action to effect dispossession or disablement of property if --

(A) there is no present right to possession of the property claimed as collateral through an enforceable security interest;

CHAPTER 10: *THE FAIR DEBT COLLECTION PRACTICES ACT*

(B) there is no present intention to take possession of the property; or

(C) the property is exempt by law from such dispossession or disablement.

(7) Communicating with a consumer regarding a debt by post card.

(8) Using any language or symbol, other than the debt collector's address, on any envelope when communicating with a consumer by use of the mails or by telegram, except that a debt collector may use his business name if such name does not indicate that he is in the debt collection business.

§ 809. Validation of debts   [15 USC 1692g]

(a) Within five days after the initial communication with a consumer in connection with the collection of any debt, a debt collector shall, unless the following information is contained in the initial communication or the consumer has paid the debt, send the consumer a written notice containing --

(1) the amount of the debt;

(2) the name of the creditor to whom the debt is owed;

(3) a statement that unless the consumer, within thirty days after receipt of the notice, disputes the validity of the debt, or any portion thereof, the debt will be assumed to be valid by the debt collector;

(4) a statement that if the consumer notifies the debt collector in writing within the thirty-day period that the debt, or any portion thereof, is disputed, the debt collector will obtain verification of the debt or a copy of a judgment against the consumer and a copy of such verification or judgment will be mailed to the consumer by the debt collector; and

(5) a statement that, upon the consumer's written request within the thirty-day period, the debt collector will provide the consumer with the name and address of the original creditor, if different from the current creditor.

(b) If the consumer notifies the debt collector in writing within the thirty-day period described in subsection (a) that the debt, or any portion thereof, is disputed, or that the consumer requests the name and address of the original creditor, the debt collector shall cease collection of the debt, or any disputed portion thereof, until the debt collector obtains verification of the debt or any copy of a judgment, or the name and address of the original creditor, and a copy of such verification or judgment, or name and address of the original creditor, is mailed to the consumer by the debt collector.

(c) The failure of a consumer to dispute the validity of a debt under this section may not be construed by any court as an admission of liability by the consumer.

§ 810. Multiple debts [15 USC 1692h]

If any consumer owes multiple debts and makes any single payment to any debt collector with respect to such debts, such debt collector may not apply such payment to any debt which is disputed by the consumer and, where applicable, shall apply such payment in accordance with the consumer's directions.

§ 811. Legal actions by debt collectors [15 USC 1692i]

(a) Any debt collector who brings any legal action on a debt against any consumer shall --

(1) in the case of an action to enforce an interest in real property securing the consumer's obligation, bring such action only in a judicial district or similar legal entity in which such real property is located; or

(2) in the case of an action not described in paragraph (1), bring such action only in the judicial district or similar legal entity --

(A) in which such consumer signed the contract sued upon; or

(B) in which such consumer resides at the commencement of the action.

(b) Nothing in this title shall be construed to authorize the bringing of legal actions by debt collectors.

§ 812. Furnishing certain deceptive forms [15 USC 1692j]

(a) It is unlawful to design, compile, and furnish any form knowing that such form would be used to create the false belief in a consumer that a person other than the creditor of such consumer is participating in the collection of or in an attempt to collect a debt such consumer allegedly owes such creditor, when in fact such person is not so participating.

(b) Any person who violates this section shall be liable to the same extent and in the same manner as a debt collector is liable under section 813 for failure to comply with a provision of this title.

§ 813. Civil liability [15 USC 1692k]

(a) Except as otherwise provided by this section, any debt collector who fails to comply with any provision of this title with respect to any person is liable to such person in an amount equal to the sum of --

(1) any actual damage sustained by such person as a result of such failure;

(2) (A) in the case of any action by an individual, such additional damages as the court may allow, but not exceeding $1,000; or

(B) in the case of a class action, (i) such amount for each named plaintiff as could be recovered under subparagraph (A), and (ii) such amount as the court may allow for all other class members, without regard to a minimum individual recovery, not to exceed the lesser of $500,000 or 1 per centum of the net worth of the debt collector; and

(3) in the case of any successful action to enforce the foregoing liability, the costs of the action, together with a reasonable attorney's fee as determined by the court. On a finding by the court that an action under this section was brought in bad faith and for the purpose of harassment, the court may award to the defendant attorney's fees reasonable in relation to the work expended and costs.

(b) In determining the amount of liability in any action under subsection (a), the court shall consider, among other relevant factors --

(1) in any individual action under subsection (a)(2)(A), the frequency and persistence of noncompliance by the debt collector, the nature of such noncompliance, and the extent to which such noncompliance was intentional; or

(2) in any class action under subsection (a)(2)(B), the frequency and persistence of noncompliance by the debt collector, the nature of such noncompliance, the resources of the debt collector, the number of persons adversely affected, and the extent to which the debt collector's noncompliance was intentional.

(c) A debt collector may not be held liable in any action brought under this title if the debt collector shows by a preponderance of evidence that the violation was not intentional and resulted from a bona fide error notwithstanding the maintenance of procedures reasonably adapted to avoid any such error.

(d) An action to enforce any liability created by this title may be brought in any appropriate United States district court without regard to the amount in controversy, or in any other court of competent jurisdiction, within one year from the date on which the violation occurs.

(e) No provision of this section imposing any liability shall apply to any act done or omitted in good faith in conformity with any advisory opinion of the Commission, notwithstanding that after such act or omission has occurred, such opinion is amended, rescinded, or determined by judicial or other authority to be invalid for any reason.

§ 814. Administrative enforcement [15 USC 1692l]

(a) Compliance with this title shall be enforced by the Commission, except to the extend that enforcement of the requirements imposed under this title is specifically committed to another agency under subsection (b). For purpose of the exercise by the Commission of its functions and powers under the Federal Trade Commission Act, a violation of this title shall be deemed an unfair or deceptive act or practice in violation of that Act. All of the functions and powers of the Commission under the Federal Trade Commission Act are available to the Commission to enforce compliance by any person with this title, irrespective of whether that person is engaged in commerce or meets any other jurisdictional tests in the Federal Trade Commission Act, including the power to enforce the provisions of this title in the same manner as if the violation had been a violation of a Federal Trade Commission trade regulation rule.

(b) Compliance with any requirements imposed under this title shall be enforced under --

(1) section 8 of the Federal Deposit Insurance Act, in the case of --

(A) national banks, by the Comptroller of the Currency;

(B) member banks of the Federal Reserve System (other than national banks), by the Federal Reserve Board; and

(C) banks the deposits or accounts of which are insured by the Federal Deposit Insurance Corporation (other than members of the Federal Reserve System), by the Board of Directors of the Federal Deposit Insurance Corporation;

(2) section 5(d) of the Home Owners Loan Act of 1933, section 407 of the National Housing Act, and sections 6(i) and 17 of the Federal Home Loan Bank Act, by the Federal Home Loan Bank Board (acting directing or through the Federal Savings and Loan Insurance Corporation), in the case of any institution subject to any of those provisions;

(3) the Federal Credit Union Act, by the Administrator of the National Credit Union Administration with respect to any Federal credit union;

(4) subtitle IV of Title 49, by the Interstate Commerce Commission with respect to any common carrier subject to such subtitle;

(5) the Federal Aviation Act of 1958, by the Secretary of Transportation with respect to any air carrier or any foreign air carrier subject to that Act; and

(6) the Packers and Stockyards Act, 1921 (except as provided in section 406 of that Act), by the Secretary of Agriculture with respect to any activities subject to that Act.

(c) For the purpose of the exercise by any agency referred to in subsection (b) of its powers under any Act referred to in that subsection, a violation of any requirement imposed under this title shall be deemed to be a violation of a requirement imposed under that Act. In addition to its powers under any provision of law specifically referred to in subsection (b), each of the agencies referred to in that subsection may exercise, for the purpose of enforcing compliance with any requirement imposed under this title any other authority conferred on it by law, except as provided in subsection (d).

(d) Neither the Commission nor any other agency referred to in subsection (b) may promulgate trade regulation rules or other regulations with respect to the collection of debts by debt collectors as defined in this title.

§ 815. Reports to Congress by the Commission [15 USC 1692m]

(a) Not later than one year after the effective date of this title and at one-year intervals thereafter, the Commission shall make reports to the Congress concerning the administration of its functions under this title, including such recommendations as the Commission deems necessary or appropriate. In addition, each report of the Commission shall include its assessment of the extent to which compliance with this title is being achieved and a summary of the enforcement actions taken by the Commission under section 814 of this title.

(b) In the exercise of its functions under this title, the Commission may obtain upon request the views of any other Federal agency which exercises enforcement functions under section 814 of this title.

§ 816. Relation to State laws [15 USC 1692n]

This title does not annul, alter, or affect, or exempt any person subject to the provisions of this title from complying with the laws of any State with respect to debt collection practices, except to the extent that those laws are inconsistent with any provision of this title, and then only to the extent of the inconsistency. For purposes of this section, a State law is not inconsistent with this title if the protection such law affords any consumer is greater than the protection provided by this title.

§ 817. Exemption for State regulation [15 USC 1692o]

The Commission shall by regulation exempt from the requirements of this title any class of debt collection practices within any State if the Commission determines that under the law of that State that class of debt collection practices is subject to requirements substantially similar to those imposed by this title, and that there is adequate provision for enforcement.

§ 818. Effective date [15 USC 1692 note]

This title takes effect upon the expiration of six months after the date of its enactment, but section 809 shall apply only with respect to debts for which the initial attempt to collect occurs after such effective date.

Approved September 20, 1977

ENDNOTES

1. So in original; however, should read "604(a)(3)."

LEGISLATIVE HISTORY:

Public Law 95-109 [H.R. 5294]

HOUSE REPORT No. 95-131 (Comm. on Banking, Finance, and Urban Affairs).

SENATE REPORT No. 95-382 (Comm. on Banking, Housing, and Urban Affairs).

CONGRESSIONAL RECORD, Vol. 123 (1977):

Apr. 4, considered and passed House.

CHAPTER 10: *THE FAIR DEBT COLLECTION PRACTICES ACT*

Aug. 5, considered and passed Senate, amended.

Sept. 8, House agreed to Senate amendment.

WEEKLY COMPILATION OF PRESIDENTIAL DOCUMENTS, Vol. 13, No. 39:

Sept. 20, Presidential statement.

AMENDMENTS:

SECTION 621, SUBSECTIONS (b)(3), (b)(4) and (b)(5) were amended to transfer certain administrative enforcement responsibilities, pursuant to Pub. L. 95-473, § 3(b), Oct. 17, 1978. 92 Stat. 166; Pub. L. 95-630, Title V. § 501, November 10, 1978, 92 Stat. 3680; Pub. L. 98-443, § 9(h), Oct. 4, 1984, 98 Stat. 708.

SECTION 803, SUBSECTION (6), defining "debt collector," was amended to repeal the attorney at law exemption at former Section (6)(F) and to redesignate Section 803(6)(G) pursuant to Pub. L. 99-361, July 9, 1986, 100 Stat. 768. For legislative history, see H.R. 237, HOUSE REPORT No. 99-405 (Comm. on Banking, Finance and Urban Affairs). CONGRESSIONAL RECORD: Vol. 131 (1985): Dec. 2, considered and passed House. Vol. 132 (1986): June 26, considered and passed Senate.

SECTION 807, SUBSECTION (11), was amended to affect when debt collectors must state (a) that they are attempting to collect a debt and (b) that information obtained will be used for that purpose, pursuant to Pub. L. 104-208 § 2305, 110 Stat. 3009 (Sept. 30, 1996).

Source: http://www.ftc.gov/

Chapter 11: Rosenthal Fair Debt Collection Practices Act (California)

CIVIL CODE
SECTION 1788-1788.3
1788. This title may be cited as the Rosenthal Fair Debt Collection Practices Act.
1.1. (a) The Legislature makes the following findings:

(1) The banking and credit system and grantors of credit to consumers are dependent upon the collection of just and owing debts. Unfair or deceptive collection practices undermine the public confidence which is essential to the continued functioning of the banking and credit system and sound extensions of credit to consumers.

(2) There is need to ensure that debt collectors and debtors exercise their responsibilities to one another with fairness, honesty and due regard for the rights of the other.

(b) It is the purpose of this title to prohibit debt collectors from engaging in unfair or deceptive acts or practices in the collection of consumer debts and to require debtors to act fairly in entering into and honoring such debts, as specified in this title.

1788.2.

(a) Definitions and rules of construction set forth in this section are applicable for the purpose of this title.

(b) The term "debt collection" means any act or practice in connection with the collection of consumer debts.

(c) The term "debt collector" means any person who, in the ordinary course of business, regularly, on behalf of himself or herself or others, engages in debt collection. The term includes any person who composes and sells, or offers to compose and sell, forms, letters, and other collection media used or intended to be used for debt collection, but does not include an attorney or counselor at law.

(d) The term "debt" means money, property or their equivalent which is due or owing or alleged to be due or owing from a natural person to another person.

CHAPTER 11: ROSENTHAL FAIR DEBT COLLECTION PRACTICES ACT (CALIF.)

(e) The term "consumer credit transaction" means a transaction between a natural person and another person in which property, services or money is acquired on credit by that natural person from such other person primarily for personal, family, or household purposes.

(f) The terms "consumer debt" and "consumer credit" mean money, property or their equivalent, due or owing or alleged to be due or owing from a natural person by reason of a consumer credit transaction.

(g) The term "person" means a natural person, partnership, corporation, limited liability company, trust, estate, cooperative, association or other similar entity.

(h) The term "debtor" means a natural person from whom a debt collector seeks to collect a consumer debt which is due and owing or alleged to be due and owing from such person.

(i) The term "creditor" means a person who extends consumer credit to a debtor.

(j) The term "consumer credit report" means any written, oral or other communication of any information by a consumer reporting agency bearing on a consumer's creditworthiness, credit standing, credit capacity, character, general reputation, personal characteristics or mode of living which is used or expected to be used or collected in whole or in part for the purpose of serving as a factor in establishing the consumer's eligibility for (1) credit or insurance to be used primarily for person, family, or household purposes, or (2) employment purposes, or (3) other purposes authorized under any applicable federal or state law or regulation. The term does not include (a) any report containing information solely as to transactions or experiences between the consumer and the person making the report; (b) any authorization or approval of a specific extension of credit directly or indirectly by the issuer of a credit card or similar device; or (c) any report in which a person who has been requested by a third party to make a specific extension of credit directly or indirectly to a consumer conveys his or her decision with respect to that request, if the third party advises the consumer of the name and address of the person to whom the request was made and such person makes the disclosures to the consumer required under any applicable federal or state law or regulation.

(k) The term "consumer reporting agency" means any person which, for monetary fees, dues, or on a cooperative nonprofit basis, regularly engages, in whole or in part, in the practice of assembling or evaluating consumer credit information or other information on consumers for the purpose of furnishing consumer credit reports to third parties, and which uses any means or facility for the purpose of preparing or furnishing consumer credit reports.

1788.3. Nothing contained in this title shall be construed to prohibit a credit union chartered under Division 5 (commencing with Section 14000) of the Financial Code or under the Federal Credit Union Act (Chapter 14 (commencing with Section 1751) of Title 12 of the United States Code) from providing information to an employer when the employer is ordinarily and necessarily entitled to receive such information because he is an employee, officer, committee member, or agent of such credit union.

Chapter 12: Form of Enterprise

You should give a lot of thought to the type of business form you choose. It would be a good idea to get professional input from a tax accountant making a decision. There are advantages and disadvantages to each. I have listed a few options below.

> A **sole proprietorship** by definition means "one owner". As owner, you assume all responsibilities.

Simplicity leads most small businesses to operate as sole proprietorships. Of course the downside is that a sole proprietorship does not have a separate legal existence apart from its owner under state law. Your DBA (doing business as) should be registered with the town or city clerk your business is located.

> A **Limited Liability Partnership** (LLP) provides liability protection for all general partners as well as management rights in the business. You have probably seen this form most frequently used by accounting firms and other professional groups.

Corporations may elect to file as a C-Corporation or S-Corporation.

> **C-Corporation** - pays federal and state income taxes on earnings. When the earnings are distributed to the shareholders as dividends, the earnings are taxed again.

> **S-Corporation** - have the same legal attributes as the C-corporation except the shareholder pays income tax on dividends via their personal income tax return.

In hindsight, I wish I had started out as a "sole proprietorship" instead of immediately forming an "S-Corporation."

I could have avoided a lot of costs and paperwork (one tax return) until I was more established and /or had reached a level requiring several employees. I should have sought out the opinion of a tax professional.

Chapter 13: Credit Reports

As a home-based enterprise on a tight budget, it may be cost prohibitive to deal directly with the three (3) major credit reporting agencies (Experian, TransUnion, Equifax) for the purpose of obtaining credit reports and reporting delinquent accounts. [See resource page for contact information]

As part of the research for this book, I contacted one of these agencies (Experian) and simply asked:

> Can a home-based collection agency (with dba filed etc) manually report their collection accounts to you assuming they did not need the ability to pull reports or require online access?

I was told: "as far as a home-based collection agency, there are a few things that have changed for residential locations. When operating out of the home, there is a $100 monthly minimum, a $200 one-time membership fee and an annual membership fee of $500.

Additionally, with the residence, a physical inspection would have to be done on the home to make sure that the office is separate from the home (meaning whatever room he/she will be working out of would have to have a lock on the door so that when done working for the day, he/she would lock the door at the end of the day like a regular business).

Unfortunately, this probably doesn't sound too attractive. What I can suggest, however, is getting signed up with an Experian reseller. They typically do not have monthly minimums and annual membership fees.

When it comes to resellers, you might want to check out First American Credco. Their web address is www.credco.com. You should be able to get set up to report with them. You can also ask them if there would be any additional cost to report to all three bureaus at the same time."

First American Credco
12395 First American Way
Poway, CA 92064
General Number (800) 255-0792

Chapter 14: Collection Techniques and Strategies

Utilize "constructive" collection techniques in your collection business by carefully evaluating each claim. Are you dealing with a "consumer" or "commercial" debt?

You should send your first demand letter on the same day the claim is received. I ALWAYS made it a practice to send a demand letter first and allowed time for delivery. A demand letter gives you a reference point when making your first phone call and eliminates any question as to when you started to work the claim.

In order to comply with the Fair Debt Collection Practices Act, you must include the following warning in your first written or verbal demand to a consumer:

> UNLESS YOU NOTIFY THIS OFFICE WITHIN 30 DAYS AFTER RECEIVING THIS NOTICE THAT YOU DISPUTE THE VALIDITY OF THIS DEBT OR ANY PORTION THEREOF, THIS OFFICE WILL ASSUME THE DEBT IS VALID. IF YOU NOTIFY THIS OFFICE IN WRITING WITHIN 30 DAYS OF RECEIVING THIS NOTICE, THIS OFFICE WILL OBTAIN VERIFICATION OF THE DEBT OR OBTAIN A COPY OF THE JUDGEMENT AND MAIL YOU A COPY OF SUCH JUDGEMENT OR VERIFICATION. IF YOU REQUEST THIS NOTICE, THIS OFFICE WILL PROVIDE YOU WITH THE NAME AND ADDRESS OF THE ORIGINAL CREDITOR. THIS LETTER IS AN ATTEMPT TO COLLECT A DEBT AND ANY INFORMATION OBTAINED WILL BE USED FOR THAT PURPOSE.

All subsequent communication to a consumer must contain the following disclosure:

> THIS IS AN ATTEMPT TO COLLECT A DEBT. ANY INFORMATION OBTAINED WILL BE USED FOR THAT PURPOSE.

CONSUMER COLLECTION TIPS

Go Easy

Listen to the debtor. Be professional. You can always get tough down the road, if the debtor makes it clear he or she has no intention of making a voluntary payment.

You will increase your chance for success by focusing on the debtor's specific situation. Contrary to popular belief, all past due debtors are not "deadbeats." If you maintain the self-esteem of the debtor, they are more likely to cooperate with you.

Don't Just Demand Payment

At times, you may be able to help resolve the situation by devising an alternate payment arrangement or simply straightening out a miscommunication between the debtor and client. Perhaps the debtor is unemployed, ill, has marital problems or disputes the contract.

DO NOT get into screaming matches. You should control the phone call. If the conversation gets out of hand and a debtor gets abusive…back off until a later time. Keep a detailed record of all information and a notation of all phone calls.

Make sure a cooperative debtor knows you appreciate their honesty and willingness to seek an amicable resolution.

• Never threaten legal action unless you plan to follow through

• Follow-up, Follow-up, Follow-up

• Send a confirmation letter

• Work towards a solution with the debtors ability to pay

• Do not make unrealistic demands

Not all collection agencies adhere to this philosophy. Many big collection agencies are "working the numbers" and have a "no excuses" perspective on collections. As a small player you are different and you will see later how this plays to your advantage over "Goliath."

CHAPTER 14: *COLLECTION TECHNIQUES AND STRATEGIES*

COMMERCIAL COLLECTION TIPS

You will want to follow the same "easy as you go" approach initially. Before going further, let's talk about:

Money and Commercial Claims

When I first started my collection agency, I wanted any business I could get. Big, small, commercial or consumer – it didn't matter. I was hungry.

You may have to do the same – but be careful not to take on huge clients, like hospitals, until you have an operation that can support such tremendous volume cost-effectively.

The following illustrates the net result of working 150 small consumer claims versus one good commercial claim.

# of accounts	Claim Amount	Agency 25%
150	$150. ea. ($4000.)	$1000.
1	$4000.	$1000.

Imagine the extra time, effort and money involved in collecting those 150 accounts. Think of the postage and follow-up communications. The phone calls. You will be lucky to collect 75 of the 150 accounts.

> Got a good commercial account – treat them like gold.

Many times when a commercial client submitted a claim they would only give me the name / address of the debtor company and a copy of the past due invoice.

Rather than pester a client. I would seek out my own detailed claim information. My local library allows patrons the opportunity to access various informational databases on-line using their library card. I would simply access business databases to ascertain the fax number and name of a contact person or owner. If possible, I also checked various state web sites to confirm information. **Total cost: $0.00.**

Armed with that information I would call the business and verify the fax number. You get fewer questions asking to "verify" a fax number than trying to "acquire" a fax number.

I would then fax my first demand notice to the business and put it to the attention of a specific individual. I was located in New York and my best client was in California. I didn't want distance to be an issue. I would follow-up the next day with a phone call to the debtor business and reference my fax transmission.

I always gave valued clients email and/or fax confirmations within 24 hours and commenced collection work within hours of claim receipt.

My "confirmations" also served as a sales tool and demonstrated the importance I placed on accounts assigned to me. Many times I had found the name of the business owner and delivered my first notice within 24 hours. Not a bad way to impress a client.

In addition to the fax transmission, I always mailed a notice to the debtor company as well.

Reality Check And General Tips

Getting several "great" commercial accounts will take time, but they are worth cultivating. I was able to collect close to $20,000 for one account over approximately 90 days...but it didn't happen over night.

When I landed a valuable commercial or consumer account, I always sent a special gift – not something with my company name on it – something personal, like a gift basket of Starbucks coffee.

How Did I Know I Had a Valuable Client?

Collection results. If the accounts being submitted were highly collectable, with some solid effort and follow-up, I felt a gift was in order. The collection of a $2000.00 claim translated to a commission of $500.00 for my agency. A nominal $25.00 appreciation gift seemed a reasonable expense.

With regards to healthcare collections, you might want to concentrate on acquiring diagnostic-related practices. It makes more sense to put your collection efforts into a $500-900 MRI type bill than a $50.00 office visit.

Also, under the Health Insurance Portability and Accountability Act of 1996 (HIPAA) you would be considered a Business Associate of a Covered Entity (the covered entity being the practice you are collecting for). You may want to consider having a Business Associate Agreement. To read more on this topic, go to: www.hipaadvisory.com

CHAPTER 14: *COLLECTION TECHNIQUES AND STRATEGIES*

Initially, you may have to take what you can get. It will all be a learning experience.

Once you gain more knowledge and your collection agency grows, you might want to consider other areas of collection such as student loans, government loans and child support. Perhaps you'll want to take a look at offering a variety of client services, such as accounts receivable management and billing. The possibilities are endless.

You should consider an arrangement with a collection attorney in your area to handle legal referrals at a pre-arranged percentage.

Depending upon claim volume and the size of the client, I sometimes recommended clients simply file a Small Claims Court action themselves. I would then agree to reduce my fee.

Rates

You must determine your own rates. I found my rates to be reasonable and rarely altered them:

> My collection rate was generally 25% of what I collected. Accounts over (1) one year old or under $75 were 50%. Second placements were 50%. Returned merchandise was 50% of normal fee.

If I had a profitable client assigning accounts on a regular basis, I would charge 25% on the first $2000.00 and 19% thereafter on a specific claim. I didn't wait for them to ask for a break. I proactively offered it as a "reward" for their business.

Chapter 15: Legal and Professional Networking

Attorney Forwarding Network

Attorney Forwarding Network was established to assist the credit and collection industry in the selection of competent and reliable out-of-town counsel for debt collection.

Source: http://www.afninc.com/

Why CollectionIndustry.com?

CollectionIndustry.com was born when Marvin Kaulkin and Mike Ginsberg, principals of Kaulkin Ginsberg Company, recognized that the information needs of the professional debt collection community were not being served on the internet.

Source: http://collectionindustry.com/

Chapter 16: Collecting Using Credit Cards

Some home-based collection agency owners have a strong enough relationship with a local bank that they can set up an account to accept credit card payments with little difficulty. I was turned down the first two times. There appears to be a concern over "charge-backs" when it comes to collection agencies.

I was eventually accepted at NBS, after clarifying the fact I was also soliciting up-to-date accounts for outsourcing. Since that time I have learned of a new company – Callipay.

Collect Using Credit Cards!

"CalliPay introduces for the first time the ability to collect using credit cards! Collection companies who have long awaited this product can now offer this convenience to their customers through CalliPay. Your customers can now charge their delinquencies on their Visa or MasterCard accounts.

CalliPay has partnered with Echo to offer you all the benefits of this new product, backed by two recognized names in the industry."

Benefits:

1. Customers can now pay you with their credit cards.

2. No equipment necessary to rent or purchase.

3. Totally Internet base. No software to buy or load.

4. Manage your credit card payments with our online reporting programmed to your needs.

5. Collect your credit card payments online with

CalliPay C-Card linked to your web-site, or via phone or fax.

Source: http://callipay.com/

Chapter 17: Sample Collection Letters and Placement Form

SAMPLE CONSUMER FIRST LETTER

Your Collection Agency
PO Box 123
Anywhere, NY 00000
(Tel)
(Fax)   Email:

> XYZ COLLECTION AGENCY IS ATTEMPTING TO COLLECT A DEBT. ANY INFORMATION OBTAINED WILL BE USED FOR THAT PURPOSE.

DATE:

Name:
Street:
City / State:

RE: Account Number:
       Amount due:
       Claimant:

The records of _____ indicate that your account is now seriously past due and that you owe the balance indicated above. Please remit this payment.

If payment has already been made, or if you desire to arrange alternate payment arrangements, contact us immediately by phone, fax, email or regular mail.

UNLESS YOU NOTIFY THIS OFFICE WITHIN 30 DAYS AFTER RECEIVING THIS NOTICE THAT YOU DISPUTE THE VALIDITY OF THIS DEBT OR ANY PORTION THEREOF, THIS OFFICE WILL ASSUME THE DEBT IS VALID. IF YOU NOTIFY THIS OFFICE IN WRITING WITHIN 30 DAYS OF RECEIVING THIS NOTICE, THIS OFFICE WILL OBTAIN VERIFICATION OF THE DEBT OR OBTAIN A COPY OF THE JUDGEMENT AND MAIL YOU A COPY OF SUCH JUDGEMENT OR VERIFICATION. IF YOU REQUEST THIS NOTICE, THIS OFFICE WILL PROVIDE YOU WITH THE NAME AND ADDRESS OF THE ORIGINAL CREDITOR. THIS LETTER IS AN ATTEMPT TO COLLECT A DEBT AND ANY INFORMATION OBTAINED WILL BE USED FOR THAT PURPOSE.

Again, if payment has already been made or you desire to arrange payment by phone, please contact us.

Yours truly,

CHAPTER 17: SAMPLE COLLECTION LETTERS AND PLACEMENT FORM

SAMPLE CONFIRMATION LETTER

Your Collection Agency
PO Box 123
Anywhere, NY 00000
(Tel)
(Fax)   Email:

> YOUR COLLECTION AGENCY IS ATTEMPTING TO COLLECT A DEBT. ANY INFORMATION OBTAINED WILL BE USED FOR THAT PURPOSE.

DATE:

Name:
Street:
City / State:

RE: Account Number:
        Amount due:
        Claimant:

This letter will serve as confirmation of your agreement to pay the above-captioned claim.

As agreed upon, [insert appropriate information concerning agreement for the full balance or payment schedule].

Please sign the enclosed extra copy of this letter and return it to us, to avoid further collection action. A postage-free return envelope has been provided for your convenience.

If you have any questions, please call.

Sincerely,

CHAPTER 17: SAMPLE COLLECTION LETTERS AND PLACEMENT FORM

SAMPLE CONSUMER FOLLOW-UP

Your Collection Agency
PO Box 123
Anywhere, NY 00000
(Tel)
(Fax)   Email:

YOUR COLLECTION AGENCY IS ATTEMPTING TO COLLECT A DEBT. ANY INFORMATION OBTAINED WILL BE USED FOR THAT PURPOSE.

DATE:

Name:
Street:
City / State:

RE: Account Number:
       Amount due:
       Claimant:

The first notice we sent you included your rights under the Fair Debt Collection Practices Act. As of the above date, neither you nor the above-captioned claimant has advised us of any dispute or of any arrangement you might have made to settle your seriously delinquent account.

Please be advised that unless payment or satisfactory resolution of your account with the above-captioned claimant is made within three (3) weeks of the date of this letter [note action to be taken such as credit bureau reporting, legal consideration etc]

If payment has already been made or if you desire to arrange payment, contact us immediately by phone, email, fax or regular mail.

Yours truly,

CHAPTER 17: SAMPLE COLLECTION LETTERS AND PLACEMENT FORM

SAMPLE COMMERCIAL NOTICE

NOTICE!

Please call, fax or email our office TODAY & advise how payment will be made.

DATE:

Attn: Officer Name
Corporate Name
Address
City / State / Zip

Amount Past Due:

ALL AMOUNTS ARE SHOWN IN US CURRENCY

Invoice copy attached for your reference and convenience.

NOTICE FOR PAYMENT!

Claimant:

Make check payable to:

Mail payment to:

Contact Information: phone / address
Email

The above claimant has retained our office to collect its claim against you. Please send the amount indicated above directly to our office.

If you have any questions concerning this claim or wish to discuss a resolution of this claim, please contact our office.

Our client values your business. However, just as you depend on an income for living expenses...our client needs to be paid for their goods and services in order to pay their own bills and stay in business.

Please remit today or call for payment arrangements.

CHAPTER 17: *SAMPLE COLLECTION LETTERS AND PLACEMENT FORM*

SAMPLE COLLECTION PLACEMENT FORM

Sample Collection Placement Form
Individual Account   (Fax or mail copies of invoices / contracts to: _____)
Your Collection Agency

Name: (Last, First): _____

Social Security Number: _____

Residence Street Add:_____ City/State/Zip:_____

Home Ph #:_____ Mail Returned: ( ) Yes ( ) No

Employer: _____

Employer Name / Address / Phone #:
_____
_____

Type of Goods Sold or Services Rendered:_____

Signed Note or Contract: ( ) YES ( ) NO Current Principal Owed: $ _____

Date of last transaction: _____

CLIENT DATA:

Date:_____ Company Name: _____

Address:_____

Contact
Person:_____

Telephone Number:_____ Email: _____

By submitting this information to us, you acknowledge and agree to the terms and
conditions that require you to report all payments, bankruptcy notices, and any
communications from the debtor directly to us upon receipt or your knowledge of
their existence. You agree to immediately stop all collection efforts on your part, and
to provide copies of any paperwork that will verify the debt, as requested by us. You
agree to pay any and all commissions owed to us. If; (1) we directly collect any
monies due to you by the debtor on this account, (2) find that the account was
previously paid by the debtor, (3) withdraw the account after demand for payment
has been made, or (4) receive any monies directly from the debtor.
NO COLLECTION - NO CHARGE.

Chapter 18: Sample Collection Service Agreement

YOUR COLLECTION AGENCY
Address
City / State / Zip

Phone / fax / email

COLLECTION SERVICE AGREEMENT

This Collection Agreement, made this _____, by and between _____, hereinafter known as "Agency," and _____, hereinafter known as "Client," sets forth the following terms and conditions:

The Agency agrees to:

- Carry out all collection efforts in compliance with all applicable federal, state, & local laws.

- Remit all monies collected to the Client along with their monthly statement.

- Collection rate is XX% of what is collected for all accounts assigned within 90 days from date of last payment or service. Collection rate is XX% of what is collected for all accounts assigned within one (1) year from date of last payment or service. Accounts over one year old or under $75 are 50%. Second placements are 50%. Returned merchandise/equipment as payment of claim: 50% of normal fee.

The Client agrees to:

- Report all payments, bankruptcy notices, and any communications from the debtor directly to the Agency upon the Client's receipt or knowledge of their existence.

- Immediately stop all collection efforts by the Client, and to provide copies of any paperwork that will verify the debt, as requested by the debtor or Agency.

- Pay any and all commission owed upon receipt of the Agency's monthly statement and pay any and all commissions owed to the Agency if:
(1) Agency directly collects any monies due to the Client by the debtor on this account,
(2) The Agency finds that the account was previously paid by the debtor,
(3) The client withdraws the account after demand for payment has been made, or
(4) The Client receives any monies directly from the debtor.

Commercial Claim – Client represents and warrants that the Creditor's claim arises out of a commercial account (a claim against a corporation, partnership or proprietorship conducted as a business venture) and that the claim is valid and lawful in all respects

SAMPLE COLLECTION SERVICE AGREEMENT (cont'd)

January 9, 2003

Information – Client warrants and represents to Your Collection Agency the truth and accuracy of information related to accounts submitted for collection.

Hold Harmless – Client shall defend, indemnify and hold harmless Your Collection Agency, its agents and employees, from and against any and all liability, loss, claims, demands, suits, actions, damages or expenses (including reasonable attorneys' fees) of every nature or description arising out of or resulting from any of the following: (a) the truth and accuracy of the information provided by Client; (b) the validity and lawfulness of Client's claim against the Debtor; (c) the Client's claim arising out of a non-commercial account; (d) any acts, omissions or claims of any attorney relating to any account forwarded by Your Collection Agency on Client's behalf for collection.

Endorsement Authorization – Client authorizes Your Collection Agency to endorse in the name of the creditor and deposit in its account any and all remittances in any form payable or endorsed to Client. Your Collection Agency is authorized to offset fees owed AGENCY from these payments. Payment's made directly to Client will be invoiced subject to the standard rates. Your Collection Agency invoice payment terms are "Payable upon receipt"

Either party upon giving _____days prior written notice to the other party may terminate this Agreement. Termination or cancellation of this agreement by either party shall have no effect on the collection, enforcement or validity of any accrued obligations owing between the parties.

This Agreement is entered into by and between AGENCY and CLIENT, this _____day of _____ 200X by their duly authorized and empowered representative(s).

Seen and agreed to as follows:

ACCEPTED:

_____

   Client Signature   Date

Print Name / Title: _____

Chapter 19: Endorsements

You're doing a professional job when clients sing your praise. Here are some excerpts of letters I have received:

A large manufacturing firm says:

"I just wanted to take a minute and tell you how satisfied we are with your company. We have been a customer of yours now for about a year, and are very pleased with the results that your company has provided us with. [Your company] has been able to collect money for approximately 9 out of every 10 customers that we have sent to them.

We usually see money in the first couple of weeks to the first month. I have only had friendly encounters with you and the employees at your company. You are always there when I have a question, and keep me up to date with every thing that is going on. Keep up the good work!"

An environmental hazards company (California) writes:

"This letter is to give thanks to your company for the help I have received with my many difficult / problem accounts. I am impressed with the quick results from the collection actions performed. My inquiries are always answered in a very timely manner and I don't feel "left in the dark" regarding the accounts that I have turned over.

I have a comfortable feeling with your company that you don't usually get with other collection agencies. I would refer your company to anybody that is in need of a good and friendly collection agency. Thanks again for your professionalism and friendliness with such difficult situations."

A (NY) precision sheet metal fabrication firm attests:

"...Ltd does not have many occasions to use a company such as yours, let me be the first to say, it was a pleasure doing business with you. You were very quick to respond to my first inquiry and once the account was placed in your hands, the service did not end. Your style of letter writing to our client was most impressive, you were professional and courteous, yet direct and to the point.

You kept us informed every step of the way, from e-mailing me to faxing copies of letters sent, as well as received from our customer. I wanted to write to express our satisfaction with you and [your company]. You can be assured that if the need arises again, we will be contacting you."

Other comments:

"You've been a great help. You gave me more information…then the other agency did in 2 years!" [client]

"Wow, I didn't think we'd get this one. Thanks for your persistence." [client]

"Thank you for working this out for them and me." [debtor]

Chapter 20: ACA International

ACA International is an international trade organization of credit and collection professionals. It provides a variety of accounts receivable management services to over on million credit grantors. Headquartered in Minneapolis, ACA serves members in the United States, Canada and 55 other countries worldwide.

Collection companies are the largest membership group under the ACA umbrella. In fact, ACA International is the largest trade association for third-party debt collection agencies. Since 1939, ACA has been serving the needs of the collection industry and has helped build it into an important aspect of our economy.

Memberships are granted through the 44 state affiliated units. The membership fees vary from state to state. Both the Unit fees and the ACA National fees are required with the membership application. The current ACA dues are $235 (includes one person) plus $20 for each additional employee; Maximum: $1,000.

Source: ACA web site - www.collector.com

Chapter 21: Resources and Vendors

Credit bureau addresses often change. Check their web sites and the Internet often for new addresses.

Equifax
http://www.equifax.com/

Experian
http://www.experian.com/

Trans Union
http://www.tuc.com/

General Business Help

The **U.S. Small Business Administration**, established in 1953, provides financial, technical and management assistance to help Americans start, run and grow their businesses.
http://www.sba.gov

Information Management

"**Accurint** can locate almost anyone, find deep background and historical information, and shorten research time and costs. Accurint provides aliases, historical addresses, relatives, associates, neighbors, assets, and more. Much more."
http://www.accurint.com

"**Skipease** was created by skiptracers and legal researchers for skiptracers and legal researchers. We are your one stop B2B skiptracing and legal research platform that's fast and free. Our site was designed for individual collectors, collection departments, legal professionals, journalists or anyone else trying to locate online skiptracing and research sources, while saving time and money."
http://www.skipease.com/

BankruptcyData.com provides instant access to information on thousands of business bankruptcy filings from federal bankruptcy districts. The database is updated daily.

CHAPTER 21: *RESOURCES AND VENDORS*

http://bankruptcydata.com/

State Trademark & Name Database
http://statetm.tripod.com/databases.htm

LawDog is a great general source of information relating to matters of general interest to the credit and collection industry.
http://lawdog.com/

Creditworthy is an internet based company providing information, products/services and programs to the Business Credit Community.
http://www.creditworthy.com/

Web Site Design, Domain Names, Hosting

"**Go Daddy Software** was started and is owned by Bob Parsons, the same guy who co-founded Parsons Technology (no longer affiliated) and who helped pioneer low cost, high performance software." Domain names, hosting, web design, transfers and much more. Great prices.
http://www.godaddy.com/

Verisign
"Build a professional site quickly and then enhance your Internet presence with VeriSign's Network Solutions line of tools and services that complement your business goals. It's easier than you think to build your own site. Let us walk you through it. You can preview your Web site before your buy. Packages include a domain name and matching e-mail, a Web site, a library of designs, and an easy site editing tool."
http://www.verisign.com/

Collection Software

"**Abacus Totality**, the Easy Collection System for Windows, is the only debt collection software specifically designed for the small office. Unlike any other collection program on the market today, it's affordable and easy to use."
http://www.abacustotality.com/

Collect! users include commercial and retail collection agencies, legal firms, credit unions, organizations with periodic billing requirements, and companies wishing to manage their receivables more effectively.
http://collect.org/

"**Collection Data Systems** (CDS) has been successfully helping collection agencies, financial institutions and the health care industry streamline their billing procedures and improve their collection of receivables with comprehensive software products."
http://collectone.com/

For more ideas – go to Google.com and search: "debt collection software" or check with the American Collectors Association (ACA).

Freelance Help

A2Zmoonlighter's web-based marketplace directly connects businesses with talented freelancers who specialize in four professional categories: IT work, Creative design work, Office administration work & Business consulting. Businesses seeking professional expertise can post their projects or contract work on A2Zmoonlighter's four specialized sites for free.
http://a2zmoonlighter.com/

bcsquared
For an innovative logo, an eye-catching brochure, or professional-looking stationery, contact Ben Carpenter of bcsquared print design.
http://www.bc2design.com

Office Supplies

"**Viking** is the leading supplier of office products to businesses throughout the world. Last year, more than 2,000,000 businesses ordered their supplies from us."
http://viking.com/

Staples: "Slashing the cost and hassle of running your office!"
http://staples.com/

Accounting

"**QuickBooks Services** help you manage your business and serve your customers more efficiently."
http://www.quickbooks.com

"**Peachtree Software** helps you better manage your accounting, your business, and your Internet presence by providing the robust features you want and the valuable insight you need!" Source:
http://www.peachtree.com/

CHAPTER 21: *RESOURCES AND VENDORS*

Credit Cards

"**CalliPay** introduces for the first time the ability to collect using credit cards! Source: http://callipay.com/

"**NBS** provides thousands of businesses nationwide with the ability to open a merchant account to accept credit card payments." Source: http://www.enbs.com/html/get_started_today.html

Printing Needs

VistaPrint eliminates the needless waste and inefficiencies of traditional low volume printing. Check them out at:
http://www.vistaprint.com/

Promotional Items

National Pen
1-800-854-1000. Great prices on more than just pens.
http://www.pens.com

About the Author

Robert Bills is a credit / collection and insurance professional with 30 years of experience. A graduate of The New School, Mr. Bills received his M.S. in Health Services Management in 1997. He earned his B.S. in Business, Management & Economics from SUNY ESC in 1994. For many years, he owned and operated a small loan company in Central New York (CNY).

He subsequently founded, a home-based collection agency providing full on-line servicing of accounts receivable for commercial, retail, medical, and business-to-business accounts.

Professional designations include: Fellow, Life Management Institute (FLMI), Life Office Management Association; Workers' Comp Law Associate (WCLA), American Educational Institute; Associate, Life & Health Claims (ALHC), International Claim Association.

Additional "works-in-progress" include: StayDestiNYUSA.com, ILoveDestiNYUSA.com, Debt2Profit.com and DangFools.com.

Disclaimer

The material in this book is not intended to be, and is not a substitute for, professional legal materials or counsel. Reasonable efforts have been made to include accurate and up-to-date information. You should not rely on the information and materials contained in this book for any purposes except as a general guide to starting a collection agency. You are responsible for seeking verification from professional legal materials and consulting independent legal counsel.